Structural Geology of the Wind River Basin, Wyoming

GEOLOGICAL SURVEY PROFESSIONAL PAPER 495-D

*Prepared in cooperation with the
Geological Survey of Wyoming and the
Department of Geology of the University of Wyoming
as part of a program of the Department of the Interior
for development of the Missouri River basin*

Structural Geology of the Wind River Basin, Wyoming

By WILLIAM R. KEEFER

GEOLOGY OF THE WIND RIVER BASIN, CENTRAL WYOMING

GEOLOGICAL SURVEY PROFESSIONAL PAPER 495-D

Prepared in cooperation with the Geological Survey of Wyoming and the Department of Geology of the University of Wyoming as part of a program of the Department of the Interior for development of the Missouri River basin

UNITED STATES GOVERNMENT PRINTING OFFICE, WASHINGTON : 1970

UNITED STATES DEPARTMENT OF THE INTERIOR

WALTER J. HICKEL, *Secretary*

GEOLOGICAL SURVEY

William T. Pecora, *Director*

For sale by the Superintendent of Documents, U.S. Government Printing Office
Washington, D.C. 20402

CONTENTS

	Page
Abstract	D1
Introduction	2
Method of study	4
Summary of stratigraphy and geologic history	6
Meaning of term "Laramide"	10
Structural geology	11
Mountain structures	11
Wind River Range	11
Washakie Range	14
Owl Creek Mountains	16
Southern Bighorn Mountains	19
Casper arch	20
Granite Mountains	20

	Page
Structural geology—Continued	
Basin structures	D22
West margin	22
North margin	23
East margin	25
South margin	25
Structural analysis	26
Foreland deformation	26
Mechanics of deformation	26
Regional uplift	29
Volcanism	30
Crustal structure and the implications of isostasy	31
References cited	33

ILLUSTRATIONS

[Plates are in pocket]

PLATE 1. Geologic map of the Wind River Basin.
          2. Structure sections across the Wind River Basin.
          3. Structure-contour map of the Wind River Basin.

	Page
FIGURE 1. Physiographic diagram of the Wind River Basin and adjacent areas in central Wyoming	D3
2–6. Thickness maps of:	
2. Paleozoic rocks	9
3. Mesozoic rocks below the Cody Shale	10
4. Cody, Mesaverde, Lewis, and Meeteetse Formations	11
5. Uppermost Cretaceous and Paleocene rocks	12
6. Lower Eocene rocks	13
7. Chart showing trends of 92 structural features in the Wind River Basin	13
8–17. Photographs showing—	
8. Dip slopes of Paleozoic and lower Mesozoic rocks along east flank of the Wind River Range	15
9. Exhumed Paleozoic rocks along Horse Creek, northwestern Wind River Basin	16
10. Precambrian gneisses, schists, and pegmatite dikes overlain by Cambrian rocks, Wind River Canyon	17
11. Vertical to overturned upper Paleozoic rocks in contact with Triassic rocks along south edge of Owl Creek Mountains	17
12. Exposure of Boysen normal fault in Wind River Canyon	19
13. Structural features along Badwater Creek, southwest end of Bighorn Mountains	21
14. Bald knobs of granite projecting above level plain of Miocene rocks, central part of Granite Mountains	22
15. Cretaceous rocks faulted against lower Eocene rocks along north side of Wind River	23
16. Folds in Indian Meadows Formation at Shotgun Butte	24
17. Intrusive mass of middle Eocene igneous rocks at Garfield Peak, central Rattlesnake Hills	25
18. Diagrams showing alternate interpretations regarding crustal movement in central Wyoming	27

CONTENTS

		Page
FIGURE	19. Diagram showing variations in density and crustal thickness required to maintain crustal equilibrium in the Wind River Basin and adjacent mountain ranges	D30
	20. Map showing relations of Bouguer gravity anomalies to regional topography and areas of thickest sequences of low-density sedimentary rocks in the Wind River Basin and surrounding mountain ranges	31
	21. Cross section showing method used in calculating amounts of Laramide uplift and subsidence	33

TABLES

		Page
TABLE	1. Selected wells drilled for oil and gas in the Wind River Basin	D4
	2. Stratigraphic units in the Wind River Basin	7
	3. Major periods of sedimentation and deformation in central Wyoming	8

GEOLOGY OF THE WIND RIVER BASIN, CENTRAL WYOMING

STRUCTURAL GEOLOGY OF THE WIND RIVER BASIN, WYOMING

By William R. Keefer

ABSTRACT

The Wind River Basin, which occupies 8,500 square miles in central Wyoming, is typical of the large sedimentary and structural basins that formed in the Rocky Mountain region during Laramide deformation. Broad belts of folded and faulted Precambrian, Paleozoic, and Mesozoic rocks surround the basin, including the Wind River Range on the west, the Washakie Range and Owl Creek and southern Bighorn Mountains on the north, the Casper arch on the east, and the Granite Mountains on the south. Relatively undeformed lower Eocene rocks occupy the central part of the basin.

Precambrian basement rocks exposed in the cores of mountain ranges indicate a long and complex history of sedimentation, plutonism, metamorphism, and deformation during Precambrian time. Rock types are chiefly granite, gneiss, and schist; abundant mafic dikes occur locally.

During Paleozoic and much of Mesozoic time, central Wyoming was part of the foreland bordering the Cordilleran geosyncline on the east. Sedimentary rocks representing all systems, except possibly the Silurian, were deposited during repeated transgressions of the epicontinental seas. Tectonic activity was limited to broad upwarping and downwarping of low amplitude along trends which in many places did not coincide with the trends of later Laramide structures. In Cretaceous time the seaways shifted eastward into eastern Wyoming in response to uplift in southeastern Idaho, and a thick sequence of alternating marine and nonmarine deposits accumulated across the Wind River Basin area.

Laramide deformation in central Wyoming began in latest Cretaceous time with downwarping of the basin trough and broad doming of parts of the peripheral areas. The intensity of movement increased through the Paleocene and culminated in earliest Eocene time in high mountains that were uplifted along reverse faults. A complete record of orogenic events is preserved in the more than 18,000 feet of fluviatile and lacustrine sediments that accumulated in the areas of greatest subsidence.

Laramide mountain-building and basin subsidence had virtually ceased by the end of early Eocene time. Clastic debris, chiefly of volcanic origin, continued to fill the basin during later Tertiary time. Near the close of the Tertiary, the entire region, mountains and basin alike, was elevated about 5,000 feet above its previous level, and the present cycle of erosion was initiated. Normal faulting, perhaps concomitant with epeirogenic uplift, resulted in the partial collapse of some Laramide uplifts.

The Wind River Basin is markedly asymmetric; the structurally deepest parts are close to the Owl Creek and Bighorn Mountains on the north and the Casper arch on the east. Asymmetry toward the southwest and a pronounced northwest alinement (N. 40° W.) of individual folds and faults dominate the structural pattern across the entire region. A geologic map, 22 structure sections, and a structure contour map drawn on top of the Paleozoic (Permian) sequence depict the principal characteristics of most structural features in the basin and surrounding mountain ranges.

Along the east flank of the Wind River Range, Paleozoic and Mesozoic strata form a linear outcrop belt with uniform northeastward (basinward) dips of 12°–15°. The monoclinal continuity is interrupted by a series of sharply folded northwest-trending anticlines which extends along the west margin of the basin for 90 miles. The 13 individual folds that occur along this trend have structural closures ranging from 500 to 4,000 feet.

The Washakie Range, at the northwest corner of the Wind River Basin, is a series of faulted folds in Precambrian, Paleozoic, and lower Mesozoic rocks that were completely buried by volcanic debris of the Absaroka Range during post-early Eocene time. The structures have now been partly exhumed along the major drainages. A continuous reverse fault probably separates the steep south flank of the range from the adjacent northwest margin of the basin.

The Owl Creek Mountains along the north margin of the Wind River Basin include a complex group of structures showing diverse trends and structural behavior. West of Mexican Pass the range is partitioned into several horstlike blocks of Precambrian rocks flanked by Paleozoic rocks. Individual blocks, trending northwest, are almost completely surrounded by reverse faults or monoclinal flexures. The adjacent basin margin is also intensely deformed into sharply folded asymmetric anticlines and synclines. East of Mexican Pass the structure of the range is virtually that of a single broad anticlinal arch with a gently dipping (12°–15°) north flank bordering the Bighorn Basin and a steep to overturned south flank that overrode the north margin of the Wind River Basin along a continuous reverse fault zone (South Owl Creek Mountains fault). Although structural relations are largely obscured by Eocene and younger strata, the available data indicate that as much as 20,000 feet of stratigraphic displacement took place along the fault zone, and that the structural relief on the upper surface of the Precambrian basement between the mountain and basin provinces locally exceeds 30,000 feet. In places the south flank of the Owl Creek Mountains was broken by numerous normal faults.

The plunging southwest end of the Bighorn Mountains forms the northeast margin of the Wind River Basin. Paleozoic and

Mesozoic strata, which dip 15°–25° basinward, have been faulted over the basin margin along the buried South Owl Creek Mountains fault. Structural relief here probably also exceeds 30,000 feet in places.

The Casper arch is a major, but not deeply eroded, structural upwarp whose steep to overturned west limb coincides with the east margin of the Wind River Basin. A nearly continuous northwest-trending series of subsidiary anticlines is superimposed along the west edge of the major arch. Drill data indicate that the South Owl Creek Mountains fault, which continues all along the west margin of the arch, has a maximum stratigraphic displacement of about 16,000 feet and maximum structural relief of about 20,000 feet.

The Granite Mountains, along the south edge of the Wind River Basin, were uplifted several thousand feet and were deeply eroded during Laramide deformation. Then, owing to extensive downfaulting and downfolding in post-early Eocene time, the central Precambrian core collapsed and was buried by middle and upper Tertiary sediments. Erosion has now exposed part of the basement complex. Both the north and south margins of the range are bounded by normal faults along which there was late Tertiary movement that caused the mountain block to be downdropped with respect to the adjacent basin areas. The west end of the range overrode the southwestern arm of the Wind River Basin along the buried Emigrant Trail reverse fault of Laramide origin. Paleozoic and Mesozoic strata dip 10°–15° N. off the north flank of the Granite Mountains, but along the basin margin these rocks were folded into several large north- and northwest-trending anticlines that project far into the interior of the basin.

The main trough of the Wind River Basin lies 3–15 miles south of the fronts of the Owl Creek and Bighorn Mountains and appears to intersect the north end of the Casper arch almost at a right angle. Altitudes on the upper surface of the Precambrian basement are as low as 24,000 feet below sea level. Subsidiary troughs occur in the eastern, southwestern, and northwestern arms of the basin. Deep drill holes reveal the presence of relatively broad folds of low amplitude in the pre-Eocene rocks along the north and east margins.

The rectilinear, asymmetric anticlinal uplifts and broad, deep synclinal basins of central Wyoming characterize the pattern of Laramide structures across the Rocky Mountain foreland region. One of the most obvious features was the involvement of the Precambrian basement and its close association with the structural development of the entire region. Whether preexisting weaknesses and inhomogeneities within the Precambrian rocks significantly influenced the location and structural configuration of Laramide features, however, is conjectural.

The development of Laramide structures in central Wyoming has been related to a vertical stress system by some geologists and to a horizontal stress system by others. The evidence is controversial, and probably no single stress system can be applied to all parts of the region or to all stages of the orogeny. The possibility of strike-slip or transverse faulting, especially along the north and south margins of the Wind River Basin, should not be overlooked, even though appreciable movements of this type cannot be demonstrated from the available data.

Laramide deformation resulted in displacements of 30,000–35,000 feet in the upper crust, requiring, according to the isostatic principle, widespread adjustments in deeper zones of the crust and upper mantle. Calculations show that, from mountain crest to mountain crest on opposite sides of the Wind River Basin, about 14,500 cubic miles of rock was uplifted and about 5,500 cubic miles of rock subsided during the orogeny. Thus, the uplift of the mountain ranges was not compensated statically by material flowing laterally from beneath the basin, or by sedimentary loading. To achieve equilibrium, enormous quantities of materials of crustal density were required at the base of the crust beneath the mountains, or else the density of the underlying mantle materials was decreased.

INTRODUCTION

The Wind River Basin in central Wyoming (fig. 1) is typical of the large sedimentary and structural basins that formed in the Rocky Mountain region during Laramide deformation. (See p. D10 for discussion of term "Laramide.") Flat-lying lower Eocene strata, part of the thick sequence of basin-fill sediments that accumulated during the major phases of tectonism in latest Cretaceous and early Tertiary times, occupy the central part of the basin. Broad belts of folded and faulted Precambrian, Paleozoic, and Mesozoic rocks, forming the flanks and cores of the adjacent mountain ranges and anticlinal complexes, completely surround it.

A systematic program of geologic mapping by the U.S. Geological Survey, begun in the early 1940's, has provided detailed stratigraphic and structural data from nearly all parts of the basin. These data, supplemented by subsurface information obtained from many hundred wells drilled for oil and gas, afford an excellent opportunity to study the time and space relations of structural features throughout this extensive crustal depression and surrounding uplifts. The tectonic evolution of the Wind River Basin is virtually analogous to that of the other large intermontane basins of Wyoming. Thus, the synthesis of regional data herein presented can be utilized in the interpretation of structure and tectonic events in other basins where present information is inadequate.

Many individuals have provided valuable information and ideas for this study; specific contributions are cited in the appropriate sections of the text. I wish, however, to cite particularly the valuable contributions of J. D. Love, which resulted not only from his own field studies in many parts of the region but also from his continuing interest and helpful advice on all phases of this basinwide study. Prof. D. L. Blackstone, Jr., Department of Geology, University of Wyoming, has likewise furnished much useful information gathered through many years of research on the geologic structure of Wyoming. T. D. Dunrud and R. L. Koogle assisted in the compilation of the geologic map (pl. 1). Dunrud also assisted in the preparation of structure contour maps for many individual oil and gas fields along the west, south, and east margins of the Wind River Basin.

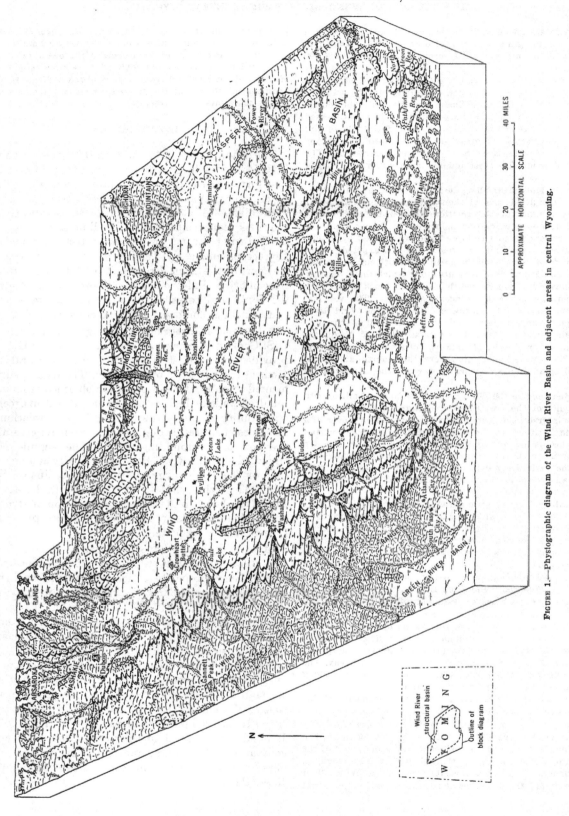

FIGURE 1.—Physiographic diagram of the Wind River Basin and adjacent areas in central Wyoming.

METHOD OF STUDY

Geologic mapping by the U.S. Geological Survey in the Wind River Basin was accomplished chiefly during the period 1945–55. Mapping was done for the most part on aerial photographs at scales generally exceeding 1:48,000 and was completed in most areas before modern 7½-minute topographic base maps became available. Consequently, many of the geologic maps of the region were compiled and published on planimetric bases. For the present study, geologic contacts were transferred from the original photographs used in field mapping to the 7½-minute (1:24,000) quadrangle maps that are now available for nearly all the basin area. These maps were then reduced photographically to the final compilation scale of 1:200,000. The present base map (pl. 1; scale 1:250,000) was compiled from parts of the Thermopolis, Arminto, Casper, and Lander Army Map Service 2° quadrangles. Because of the small scale, it was necessary in several cases to combine closely related formations into single stratigraphic units on both the geologic map and structure sections.

Twenty-two structure sections (pl. 2) were constructed to show the major geologic features in the basin and surrounding uplifts. Most were drawn through, or near, key wells for maximum subsurface control (see table 1 for list of wells). The small scale requires generalization of many small features. Some of the anticlines, for example, that are shown as simple folds are known from drill data to contain numerous minor faults at depth. All sections were drawn to the top of the Precambrian basement complex, the stratigraphic thicknesses of overlying rocks being determined from regional isopach maps (figs. 2–6) in areas where drill data are not available.

TABLE 1.—*Selected wells drilled for oil and gas in the Wind River Basin, Wyoming*

A. Wells used in construction of cross sections, plate 2 and compilation of structure contour map, plate 3

No. on pls. 2, 3	Company	Well	Sec.	Township	Range	Projected into line of section from—
C-1	Davis Oil Co	Bermingham 1	SW¼NE¼ 2	41 N.	106 W.	
2	Shell Oil Co	Goose Lake 1	NW¼SE¼ 9	42 N.	105 W.	
E-1	Trigood Oil Co	Tribal 1	NW¼SW¼ 21	6 N.	3 W.	0.3 mile west.
F-1	British-American Oil Producing Co.	Q-1	NW¼SW¼ 30	4 N.	1 W.	
2	do	Tribal C-14	NE¼SE¼ 30	4 N.	1 W.	0.2 mile southeast.
G-1	Shell Oil Co	Gov't.-Tribal 33×10	NW¼SE¼ 10	3 N.	2 E.	1.2 miles east.
2	Gulf Oil Corp	Mae Rhodes 1	SW¼SW¼ 3	3 N.	2 E.	
3	El Paso Natural Gas	Hornbeck-Govt. 1	NE¼SW¼ 19	4 N.	3 E.	2.2 miles east.
H-1	Pan American Petroleum Corp.	Tribal 1	NE¼NE¼ 34	1 N.	2 E.	0.5 mile west.
2	do	do	NE¼SW¼ 24	1 N.	2 E.	Do.
3	Phillips Petroleum Co	Missouri 1	NW¼SE¼ 8	2 N.	4 E.	
4	Pan American Petroleum Corp.	Tribal 1	NW¼SE¼ 11	5 N.	4 E.	
I-1	Sinclair Oil and Gas Co	Federal 2-646-Fremont	NW¼NW¼ 10	33 N.	97 W.	0.8 mile southeast.
2	Atlantic Refining Co	Tribal 4	SW¼SW¼ 36	1 S.	4 E.	
3	do	Tribal 6	SW¼SW¼ 30	1 S.	5 E.	0.3 mile northwest.
4	Stanolind Oil and Gas Co	Tribal C-1	SW¼SE¼ 1	1 S.	5 E.	0.2 mile northwest.
5	Continental Oil Co	Tribal 1	SE¼SE¼ 1	1 S.	5 E.	
6	Farmers Union	do	SE¼SE¼ 28	1 N.	6 E.	
J-1	Quest Oil Co	Quest-Govt. 1	SE¼NW¼ 14	31 N.	99 W.	Do.
2	Routt Oil Co	Lowe 3	SW¼SW¼ 33	32 N.	98 W.	0.3 mile southeast.
3	Continental Oil Co	Govt. 2	SE¼SE¼ 8	32 N.	97 W.	0.8 mile southeast.
4	Pan American Petroleum Corp.	Unit 52	NE¼SE¼ 9	33 N.	96 W.	
5	do	Unit 34 M	NW¼NW¼ 10	33 N.	96 W.	0.2 mile southeast.
6	do	Unit 12 F	NW¼SE¼ 3	33 N.	96 W.	
7	do	Unit 33 L	NE¼NW¼ 2	33 N.	96 W.	0.3 mile southeast.
8	Atlantic Refining Co	Tribal A-1	SE¼SE¼ 29	1 S.	6 E.	
K-1	West Sand Draw Syndicate	Govt. 1	SW¼SW¼ 20	32 N.	95 W.	0.3 mile northwest.
2	Sinclair-Wyoming Oil Co	Unit 8-C	SE¼SE¼ 15	32 N.	95 W.	
3	do	Unit 5	NE¼SW¼ 14	32 N.	95 W.	
4	Ryan Oil Co	Burley Dome 1	NW¼SE¼ 5	32 N.	94 W.	
L-1	Wind River Oil Co	Hagood Govt. 1	NE¼SW¼ 23	34 N.	95 W.	0.2 mile west.
M-1	Champlin Oil & Refining Co	Federal-Caster	SE¼SW¼ 29	31 N.	94 W.	
2	Pan American Petroleum Corp.	Unit 1	SW¼NE¼ 22	31 N.	94 W.	
3	Forest Oil Corp	Govt. 11-1	NE¼NE¼ 11	33 N.	94 W.	0.8 mile west.
4	Circle A Drilling Co., Inc	Federal 1	SE¼SE¼ 7	34 N.	93 W.	0.7 mile east.
5	Superior Oil Co	Fuller Reservoir 1-26	NW¼SE¼ 26	36 N.	94 W.	2 miles west.
6	Humble Oil & Refining Co	Poison Creek 1	NE¼NE¼ 32	37 N.	93 W.	0.5 mile west.
7	do	Poison Creek 2	NE¼NE¼ 17	37 N.	93 W.	0.7 mile west.
8	California Co	Reynolds 1	SW¼NE¼ 10	38 N.	93 W.	0.5 mile east.

TABLE 1.—*Selected wells drilled for oil and gas in the Wind River Basin, Wyoming*—Continued

A. Wells used in construction of cross sections, plate 2 and compilation of structure contour map, plate 3—Continued

No. on pls. 2, 3	Company	Well	Location Sec.	Township	Range	Projected into line of section from—
M-9	Shell Oil Co	Unit 23-15	NE¼SW¼ 15	39 N.	93 W.	
N-1	Carter Oil Co	Emigrant Trail	SE¼NW¼ 32	30 N.	93 W.	
2	Fresco Exploration Co	Govt. 1	NW¼NW¼ 28	32 N.	91 W.	0.6 mile east.
3	Pan American Petroleum Corp.	USA-Cheney 1	NE¼NE¼ 17	32 N.	91 W.	0.2 mile east.
4	Davis Oil Co	Govt.-Grieve 1	SW¼SW¼ 34	33 N.	91 W.	0.5 mile east.
5	Empire State Oil Co	State 2	NE¼NW¼ 16	33 N.	91 W.	0.3 mile west.
6	A. Edmiston	Govt. 1	NW¼NW¼ 26	35 N.	91 W.	0.9 mile east.
7	Continental Oil Co	Love Ranch 1	NE¼SE¼ 11	35 N.	91 W.	1.4 miles east.
8	do	Unit 14-4	NW¼NW¼ 14	36 N.	91 W.	0.6 mile east.
9	do	Moneta Hills 11-1	NE¼SE¼ 11	37 N.	91 W.	
10	True Oil Co	Garvin 1	NE¼SE¼ 14	38 N.	91 W.	
11	California Co	Hugh Day 1	SW¼NW¼ 12	38 N.	91 W.	0.2 mile east.
12	Sinclair-Wyoming Oil Co	Lysite 1	NW¼NW¼ 35	39 N.	91 W.	0.8 mile west.
13	Gulf Oil Corp	Lysite-Federal 1	SW¼NE¼ 23	39 N.	91 W.	0.6 mile east.
O-1	Morton	Unit 1	SE¼NE¼ 13	33 N.	90 W.	0.5 mile west.
2	Davis Oil Co	Govt. 1	NW¼NW¼ 30	34 N.	89 W.	0.7 mile west.
3	Continental Oil Co	Squaw Butte 23-3	NW¼NW¼ 23	36 N.	89 W.	2.0 miles east.
4	Humble Oil & Refining Co	Frenchie Draw 1	NE¼NE¼ 21	37 N.	89 W.	0.5 mile east.
5	Pure Oil Co	Badwater 2-A	NE¼NW¼ 2	38 N.	89 W.	
6	do	Badwater 1	NE¼NE¼ 35	39 N.	89 W.	
P-1	Forest Oil Corp	Forest 20-1	NE¼NE¼ 20	34 N.	88 W.	0.3 mile east.
2	C. E. Brehm	Govt. 1	SW¼SW¼ 4	34 N.	88 W.	0.4 mile east.
3	Humble Oil & Refining Co	Govt.-Witt 1	NE¼NE¼ 24	36 N.	88 W.	1.8 miles east.
4	Superior Oil Co	Unit 14-29	SW¼SW¼ 29	38 N.	87 W.	0.2 mile east.
Q-1	Davis Oil Co	Unit 1	NE¼NE¼ 26	34 N.	88 W.	0.7 mile west.
2	Sunray Mid-Continent Oil Co	Federal C-1	NE¼SE¼ 13	35 N.	88 W.	1.6 miles west.
3	California Co	Cooper Reservoir 3	SE¼SW¼ 4	35 N.	87 W.	
4	do	Cooper Reservoir 1	SE¼SW¼ 3	35 N.	87 W.	0.9 mile east.
5	do	Cooper Reservoir 2	SE¼SW¼ 34	36 N.	87 W.	0.4 mile east.
6	do	Waltman 2	NW¼SE¼ 1	36 N.	87 W.	0.2 mile east.
7	do	Waltman 1	NE¼SW¼ 31	37 N.	86 W.	0.3 mile west.
8	Pure Oil Co	do	SW¼NW¼ 29	37 N.	86 W.	
R-1	Cities Service Oil Co	Govt. 1	NW¼NW¼ 7	33 N.	87 W.	0.2 mile northwest.
2	Padon Co	do	NW¼NW¼ 8	33 N.	87 W.	0.6 mile southeast.
3	California Co	Twidale 1	NE¼NE¼ 28	34 N.	87 W.	0.3 mile northwest.
4	National Corp. Refining Assoc.	Unit 1	SE¼NW¼ 22	34 N.	87 W.	0.4 mile northwest.
5	Bay Petroleum Corp	do	SW¼NE¼ 15	34 N.	87 W.	0.9 mile northwest.
6	Humble Oil & Refining Co	Unit 2	NE¼NW¼ 14	35 N.	86 W.	
7	Farmers Union Central Exchange, Inc.	Govt. Ames 1	SE¼SW¼ 28	36 N.	85 W.	0.6 mile southeast.
S-1	True Oil Co	Sun Ranch 1	NE¼SE¼ 30	34 N.	85 W.	
2	British-American Oil Producing Co.	Eccles 1	SE¼SE¼ 31	35 N.	84 W.	0.2 mile southeast.
3	do	Govt. Downer 1	SE¼NE¼ 31	35 N.	84 W.	0.1 mile northwest.
T-1	Forest Oil Corp	Unit 3-28-1	NE¼SE¼ 28	32 N.	85 W.	
2	do	Govt. 18-22-10	SE¼SE¼ 22	32 N.	85 W.	
3	Cities Service Oil Co	Govt. C-1	NW¼SW¼ 12	32 N.	85 W.	0.1 mile southeast.
4	Pure Oil Co	West Poison Spider 1	NW¼SE¼ 11	33 N.	84 W.	
5	Empire State Oil Co	T-2	NW¼NW¼ 33	34 N.	83 W.	
U-1	Chicago Corp	Govt. Tysor 2c	SW¼SW¼ 2	31 N.	84 W.	
2	Tidewater Assoc. Oil Co	Unit 1	SE¼NE¼ 31	32 N.	83 W.	
3	Texas Co	do	NE¼SW¼ 35	33 N.	82 W.	

B. Additional wells used in compilation of structure contour map, plate 3

[Wells in developed oil and gas fields not shown]

No. on pl. 3	Company	Well	Location Section	Township	Range	Total depth (feet)
1	California Co	Govt.-Langguth 1	SW¼SW¼ 6	42 N.	107 W.	5,329
2	Davis Oil Co	McCulloch-Govt. 1	SW¼SW¼ 21	42 N.	107 W.	2,930
3	Franco-Western Oil Co	Govt. 55-34	NW¼SE¼ 34	43 N.	107 W.	3,392
4	do	Unit 7-2	SW¼SE¼ 2	42 N.	107 W.	2,566
5	True Oil Co	Unit 1	SW¼NE¼ 8	42 N.	106 W.	5,262
6	Carter Oil Co	State 1	NW¼NE¼ 17	41 N.	105 W.	5,056
7	Shell Oil Co	Tribal 1	NE¼NE¼ 30	7 N.	5 W.	8,001
8	Lamar Hunt	do	SW¼NW¼ 18	6 N.	3 W.	5,119

TABLE 1.—*Selected wells drilled for oil and gas in the Wind River Basin, Wyoming*—Continued

B. Additional wells used in compilation of structure contour map, plate 3—Continued

[Wells in developed oil and gas fields not shown]

No. on pl. 3	Company	Well	Location Section	Township	Range	Total depth (feet)
9	Cities Service Oil Co	do	NE¼SW¼ 9	5 N.	1 E.	10,905
10	Phillips Petroleum Co	Boysen 1	SE¼SE¼ 27	5 N.	5 E.	15,050
11	Mobil Oil Co	F-33-6-I	NW¼SE¼ 6	1 N.	6 E.	9,001
12	do	F-33-14-G	NW¼SE¼ 14	37 N.	94 W.	12,839
13	Shell Oil Co	Unit 22-27	SE¼NW¼ 27	35 N.	93 W.	8,012
14	Seaboard Oil Co	Double Butte 1	SE¼SW¼ 2	34 N.	93 W.	5,030
15	John F. Camp	Govt. 3	NW¼SW¼ 26	33 N.	93 W.	2,679
16	Far West Oil Co	Govt.-Sande 1	NW¼SE¼ 5	32 N.	93 W.	3,627
17	Oil Capitol Corp	Govt. 1	SW¼NW¼ 12	32 N.	93 W.	7,378
18	McCulloch Oil Co	Govt-Voth 1	SW¼NE¼ 26	39 N.	92 W.	11,210
19	George Anderman	Govt. 1	NE¼SW¼ 3	37 N.	92 W.	10,007
20	Carter Oil Co	Govt.-Walker 1	NE¼NW¼ 33	37 N.	92 W.	7,242
21	Humble Oil & Refining Co	Sand Hills 2	SE¼SW¼ 11	36 N.	92 W.	8,451
22	Quintana Production Co	Hawkins Draw 1	SE¼SE¼ 18	35 N.	92 W.	8,960
23	Sinclair Oil Co	Muskrat A-5	SW¼SW¼ 34	34 N.	92 W.	7,620
24	Pan-American Petroleum Corp	USA-Deuel 1	NW¼SW¼ 35	33 N.	92 W.	6,103
25	do	USA-Chorney 1	SE¼SE¼ 3	32 N.	92 W.	4,930
26	California Co	State 1	NE¼SE¼ 4	38 N.	91 W.	11,528
27	Anchutz Oil Co	Govt. 1	SE¼SE¼ 2	34 N.	91 W.	7,200
28	Sinclair Oil Co	Federal-Travis 1	SE¼SW¼ 13	34 N.	91 W.	2,980
29	McCulloch Oil Co	Govt.-Cole 1	NW¼NW¼ 31	39 N.	90 W.	9,520
30	California Co	R. W. Spratt & Sons 1	SE¼SE¼ 5	38 N.	90 W.	8,987
31	Pan American Petroleum Corp	Moneta Hills 1	SE¼SE¼ 31	38 N.	90 W.	11,655
32	Humble Oil & Refining Co	Frenchie Draw 2-B	NE¼NE¼ 21	37 N.	90 W.	11,340
33	Continental Oil Co	Squaw Butte 1-2	NE¼SE¼ 1	36 N.	90 W.	8,656
34	do	Squaw Butte 28-1	NW¼NW¼ 28	36 N.	90 W.	6,956
35	do	Squaw Butte 26-5	SE¼SE¼ 26	36 N.	90 W.	8,015
36	Shell Oil Co	Unit 1	NW¼SE¼ 16	35 N.	90 W.	8,017
37	Richfield Oil Corp	Travis 1	NW¼NW¼ 31	34 N.	90 W.	7,745
38	Superior Oil Co	Govt-Davis 81-4	NE¼NE¼ 4	33 N.	90 W.	6,112
39	Sinclair Oil Co	Unit 1	SE¼NE¼ 22	33 N.	90 W.	3,418
40	California Co	Govt. 1	NE¼SW¼ 8	38 N.	89 W.	12,505
41	Continental Oil Co	Unit 1	SE¼SE¼ 36	35 N.	89 W.	6,848
42	Champlin Oil Co	Raderville 5	NE¼SE¼ 1	34 N.	89 W.	4,159
43	Lubar Oil Co	Unit 1	SW¼SW¼ 23	34 N.	89 W.	4,010
44	Superior Oil Co	Unit 34-25	SW¼SW¼ 25	34 N.	89 W.	2,600
45	Humble Oil & Refining Co	Hiland 2	SE¼NW¼ 32	37 N.	88 W.	10,250
46	Stuckenoff Oil Co	Govt. 1	SW¼SW¼ 19	34 N.	88 W.	957
47	Shell Oil Co	Aspirin Creek 11-22	NW¼NW¼ 25	35 N.	87 W.	8,000
48	Cities Service Oil Co	Unit 1	SE¼SW¼ 14	33 N.	87 W.	6,145
49	Brinkerhoff Drilling Co	Govt. 1	NW¼SE¼ 24	33 N.	87 W.	6,008
50	Continental Oil Co	Hells Half Acre 1	NW¼SE¼ 22	36 N.	86 W.	9,011
51	Gage Oil & Gas Co	Humble-State 1	E½SE¼ 36	33 N.	86 W.	9,093
52	Sun Oil Co	Chorney-Wolf Govt. 1	SE¼NW¼ 27	33 N.	85 W.	6,500
53	Shell Oil Co	Unit 33-5	NW¼SE¼ 5	31 N.	84 W.	4,236
54	Atlantic Refining Co	Unit 1	SW¼SE¼ 5	31 N.	84 W.	1,949
55	Colorado Oil & Gas Corp	do	SW¼NW¼ 15	31 N.	84 W.	3,492

Most petroleum geologists have drawn structure contours on top of the Lower Cretaceous Cloverly Formation ("Dakota" of petroleum geologists) because this unit provides a distinctive reflecting horizon for seismic surveys. Inasmuch as the Cloverly has been stripped away by erosion around much of the basin margin, however, the top of the Permian System (table 2, Ervay Member locally of the Park City Formation and locally of the Goose Egg Formation) was selected to best portray the structure of the region for purposes of this report (pl. 3). Remnants of Permian rocks are still preserved across the crests of most of the marginal anticlines, and the structural configurations can be worked out in detail from the many wells that penetrate the horizon at depth. The structure contour map was drawn subsequent to the preparation of the cross sections (pl. 2); thus, it is based chiefly on elevations at the top of the Permian sequence as shown on those sections.

SUMMARY OF STRATIGRAPHY AND GEOLOGIC HISTORY

Detailed descriptions of stratigraphic units in the Wind River Basin have been given in many published papers, and only a summary discussion is included in this report (table 2). The reader is referred to the following publications for regional stratigraphic data: (1) Paleozoic rocks—Keefer and Van Lieu (1966); (2) Mesozoic rocks—Love, Johnson, Nace, and others (1945); Love, Thompson, Johnson, and others (1945);

TABLE 2.—*Stratigraphic units in the Wind River Basin, Wyoming*

Age	Unit	Thickness (feet)	Dominant lithology	Remarks
Quaternary	Surficial deposits	0–10+	Unconsolidated sand and gravel deposits in terraces, pediments, glacial moraines, and valley alluvium.	
Pliocene	Moonstone Formation	0–1,350	Claystone, shale, and tuffaceous sandstone; some conglomerate and limestone.	Confined to central part of Granite Mountains.
Miocene	Split Rock Formation [1]	0–3,000	Tuffaceous sandstone and conglomerate.	Confined to area south of Beaver Divide.
Oligocene	White River Formation	0–800	Widespread conglomerate at base overlain by tuffaceous siltstone, claystone, and sandstone.	Confined to Beaver Divide area.
	Wiggins Formation	0–3,000	Volcanic conglomerate and tuffaceous sandstone.	Confined to Absaroka Range.
Eocene — Middle and late	Wagon Bed Formation	0–700	Arkosic sandstone and conglomerate; tuffaceous siltstone, claystone, and sandstone.	Confined to Beaver Divide area.
	Tepee Trail and Aycross Formations	0–2,500	Volcanic conglomerate, tuffaceous sandstone and claystone.	Confined to north margin of basin.
Eocene — Early	Wind River Formation	0–9,000	Sandstone, conglomerate, siltstone, and claystone.	Forms surface rock over much of basin area.
	Indian Meadows Formation		Conglomerate, sandstone, and siltstone.	
Paleocene	Fort Union Formation	0–8,000	Sandstone, siltstone, and shale.	
Cretaceous — Late	Lance Formation	0–6,000	Sandstone, shale, and claystone.	
	Meeteetse Formation	200–1,335	Sandstone, siltstone, carbonaceous shale, and coal.	Contains tongues of marine Lewis shale in eastern part of basin.
	Mesaverde Formation	700–2,000	Sandstone, siltstone, carbonaceous shale, and coal.	
	Cody Shale	3,600–5,000	Shale in lower half; shaly sandstone and shale in upper half.	
	Frontier Formation	600–1,000	Sandstone and shale.	
Cretaceous — Early	Mowry Shale	250–700	Shale and bentonite.	
	Thermopolis Shale	125–250	Shale; Muddy Sandstone Member at top contains sandstone and minor amount of shale.	
	Cloverly and Morrison Formations.	200–700	Sandstone, claystone, and lenticular conglomerate.	Systemic boundary may be 100–200 ft above base.
Jurassic	Sundance Formation	200–550	Sandstone, limestone, and shale.	
	Gypsum Spring Formation	0–250	Limestone, shale, claystone, and gypsum.	
Jurassic(?) and Triassic(?)	Nugget Sandstone	0–500	Sandstone; some shale in lower part.	
Triassic	Chugwater Group	1,000–1,300	Siltstone, shale, and sandstone; Alcova Limestone is a thin (max 15 ft) persistent unit 800–1,000 ft above base.	
	Dinwoody Formation	50–200	Siltstone, shale, and sandstone.	
Permian	Park City Formation (Goose Egg Formation)	350–380	Shale and gypsum; some thin beds of limestone.	Present in eastern third of basin.
		200–400	Limestone, chert, sandstone, and siltstone.	Ervay Member at top is structure contour horizon.
Pennsylvanian	Tensleep Sandstone	200–600	Sandstone.	Casper Formation (Pennsylvanian and Permian) in southeastern part of basin.
	Amsden Formation	0–400	Sandstone at base, overlain by limestone, dolomite, and shale.	Absent in southeastern part of basin.
Mississippian	Madison Limestone	300–700	Limestone.	
Devonian	Darby Formation	0–300	Dolomite, limestone, shale, and siltstone.	Absent in east half of basin.
Ordovician	Bighorn Dolomite	0–300	Dolomite.	Absent in east half of basin.
Cambrian	Gallatin Limestone	0–365	Limestone.	Absent in southeast corner of basin.
	Gros Ventre Formation	0–700	Shale, limestone, and shaly sandstone.	Absent in southeast corner of basin.
	Flathead Sandstone	50–500	Sandstone and quartzite.	
Precambrian	Igneous and metamorphic rocks		Granite, granite gneiss, schist, and metasedimentary rocks.	Exposed along crests of mountain ranges.

[1] Since this report was prepared, the name "Split Rock Formation" has been abandoned and replaced by the name "Arikaree Formation."

Love, Tourtelot, Johnson, and others (1945, 1947), Thompson, Love, and Tourtelot (1949), Yenne and Pipiringos (1954), and Keefer and Rich (1957); (3) uppermost Cretaceous, Paleocene, and lower Eocene rocks—Keefer (1965a); (4) middle and upper Tertiary rocks—Love (1939, 1970), Tourtelot (1957), Keefer (1957), Rich (1962), and Van Houten (1964). Major periods of sedimentation and deformation are given in table 3.

TABLE 3.—*Major periods of sedimentation and deformation in central Wyoming*

Geologic time interval	Duration (million years)	Tectonic behavior	Sedimentation per million years (feet)
Cambrian to latest Cretaceous.	500	Predominantly subsidence, interrupted periodically by broad upwarping of certain areas.	20–30
Latest Cretaceous to end of early Eocene.	25	Intense deformation; development of great folds and downwarps with amplitudes exceeding 30,000 ft.	720 (max.)
Middle Eocene to middle Pliocene.	40	Relative quiescence; little differential movement between mountains and basins.	100–150
Middle Pliocene to Recent.	10	Regional uplift of about 5,000 ft; normal faulting resulting in collapse of some mountain blocks a few hundred to a few thousand feet.	(Basin-fill sediments eroded.)

Igneous and metamorphic rocks of Precambrian age form the cores of mountain ranges along the south, west, and north sides of the Wind River Basin (pl. 1). Although widely exposed, the basement complex has been studied in detail only locally (Love, 1939, p. 13–14; McLaughlin, 1940; Wise, 1964, p. 292–297; Parker, 1962; Worl, 1963, 1967; Bayley, 1965 a–d; Love, 1970). Granite, granite gneiss, and schist are the predominant rock types; locally, there are abundant mafic dikes. Relationships within the basement indicate a long, complex, and poorly understood history of sedimentation, plutonism, metamorphism, and deformation during Precambrian time.

Central Wyoming was tectonically stable in later Precambrian time and became part of the eastern foreland of the Cordilleran geosyncline. Extensive erosion reduced the region to a broad, nearly level, plain before the initial advance of the epicontinental sea in Middle Cambrian time.

Central Wyoming remained a part of the foreland throughout Paleozoic and much of Mesozoic time. Sediments representing all systems, except possibly the Silurian, were deposited during repeated transgressions of the seas (table 2), but the stratigraphic sequence is thin and discontinuous as compared to the thick geosynclinal accumulations farther west in Idaho (Armstrong and Oriel, 1965, p. 1849–1855). Deposition occurred mainly in shallow seas; therefore slight changes in base level, caused by fluctuations in sea level or by tectonic movements of low amplitude, resulted in many widespread unconformities and changes in the patterns of sedimentation (Keefer, 1965b). Periodically, some areas were raised above the level of the sea, and were eroded. Most Paleozoic and early Mesozoic structural features seem to bear little resemblance to features developed later during Laramide deformation.

Paleozoic strata consist chiefly of resistant limestone, dolomite, and sandstone (table 2); total thickness increases from about 1,200 feet in the southeastern part of the Wind River Basin to more than 3,200 feet in the northwestern part (fig. 2). Mesozoic strata are predominantly shale, siltstone, and sandstone. These rocks (exclusive of the uppermost Cretaceous Lance Formation) also thicken westward from 8,500 feet along the east margin of the basin to an estimated 11,500 feet along the west margin (figs. 3, 4).

In latest Jurassic or earliest Cretaceous time, highlands formed in the geosynclinal area of southeastern Idaho (Armstrong and Oriel, 1965, p. 1854), and the major sites of deposition shifted eastward. By Late Cretaceous time the main seaways had migrated into eastern Wyoming, and a thick sequence of alternating transgressive, regressive, and nonmarine deposits accumulated across central Wyoming. The latest Cretaceous marine invasion (represented by the Lewis Shale) covered only the eastern part of the Wind River Basin.

Little tectonic activity occurred in the basin area during the period of Meeteetse and Lewis deposition, although thickness variations in places indicate ancestral folding of some anticlines and synclines (Keefer and Troyer, 1964, p. 28–31). Most of the Laramide deformation, however, postdates the Meeteetse and Lewis; the upper surface of these two formations may therefore be used as a convenient datum plane of deformation. At this time the top of the Precambrian basement lay about 10,000 feet below sea level in the eastern part of the Wind River Basin and 15,000 feet in the western part, and had an average westward dip of about 40 feet per mile. This basement surface forms a reference for calculating the magnitude of basin sinking and mountain uplift during successive stages of the orogeny.

Major Laramide deformation began in latest Cretaceous time (beginning of Lance deposition) with pronounced downwarping of the basin trough and broad doming of parts of the peripheral areas. The intensity of movement increased through the Paleocene and cul-

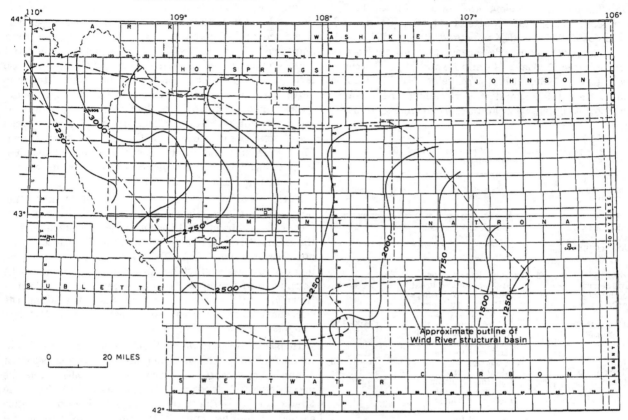

FIGURE 2.—Thickness map of Paleozoic rocks, Wind River Basin. Isopach interval 250 feet. Isopachs are restored across mountain arches where rocks have been eroded.

minated in earliest Eocene time as high mountains were uplifted along reverse faults.[1] Clastic debris, stripped from the flanks of the rising mountain arches, was shed basinward from all sides. A complete record of orogenic events is preserved in the more than 18,000 feet of fluviatile and lacustrine sediments of the Lance, Fort Union, Indian Meadows, and Wind River Formations (see table 2; figs. 5, 6) that accumulated in the areas of greatest subsidence (Keefer, 1965a, p. A55–A58). By the end of early Eocene time, the basin-fill lapped high onto the mountain flanks and probably buried the Casper arch and parts of the Owl Creek Mountains and the Washakie Range.

Basin subsidence and mountain elevation had virtually ended by the close of the early Eocene. Renewed folding and faulting of existing structural features (for example, Casper arch) took place after deposition of the Wind River Formation, but with few exceptions these movements were of minor consequence and did not greatly modify the structural patterns that had already been established.

Extensive sedimentation thickened the fill of the Wind River Basin in middle and late Tertiary times (Love, 1970). The middle and upper Eocene, Oligocene, Miocene, and Pliocene rocks are predominantly volcanic (table 2), in sharp contrast to the predominantly nonvolcanic, locally derived clastic material of the lower Eocene and older parts of the basin fill. The volcanic debris was derived in large part from the great Yellowstone-Absaroka volcanic field at the northwest corner of the basin, and, locally, from a smaller center in the Rattlesnake Hills in the southeastern part of the basin (figs. 1, 17). By Pliocene time apparently only the highest mountain ridges projected above the sedimentary plain. Then, perhaps in middle or late Pliocene time, the entire region, mountains and basin alike, was uplifted several thousand feet, the cycle was reversed, and a long period of degradation began and still continues. Re-excavation has now progressed to the point where only the lower Eocene and older rocks still remain in the central part of the basin. Large-scale normal faulting, probably

---

[1] In this report, the terms "reverse faults" and "thrust faults" are used interchangeably for those faults in which the hanging wall has moved up relative to the footwall. The term "normal fault" is used for those faults in which the hanging wall has moved down with respect to the footwall. A high-angle fault has a dip greater than 45°, and a low-angle fault has a dip less than 45°.

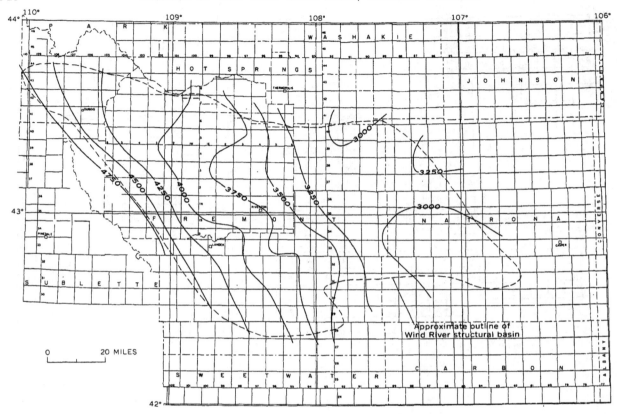

FIGURE 3.—Thickness map of Mesozoic rocks below the Cody Shale (lower Upper Cretaceous), Wind River Basin. Isopach interval 250 feet. Isopachs are restored across mountain arches where rocks have been eroded.

closely related to regional uplift, also occurred in late Tertiary time. In many places this faulting resulted in the partial collapse of major Laramide uplifts near, or along, older reverse fault zones.

MEANING OF TERM "LARAMIDE"

The term "Laramide" has long been applied to a period of large-scale crustal disturbances during which the mountains and basins of the Rocky Mountain region were formed. Wilmarth (1938, p. 1149) defined the Laramide as beginning in Late Cretaceous time and ending in early Tertiary time, thus relating it to the time span represented by the so-called Laramie Formation of pioneer geologists in the eastern part of the region. As more structural data accumulate, however, it is increasingly evident that orogenic events presently ascribed to the Laramide did not begin nor end simultaneously in all parts of the Rocky Mountains. Structural features developed in response to a wave of tectonism that began in the geosynclinal area to the west before Cretaceous time, and deformation of various kinds, as well as volcanism, proceeded periodically in some parts of the Rocky Mountains until middle or even late Tertiary time. The evidence is well documented in many published papers, and will not be reviewed here. It is sufficient to note that at present there is controversy regarding the time limits that should be placed on the orogeny, and the events that should be related to it.

The present study of structural features in the Wind River Basin and associated mountain ranges suggests that the limits and scope of the Laramide can best be defined in terms of basin development, which was a most important part of the orogenic process in central Wyoming. Subsidence of the major basin trough began in latest Cretaceous (Lance) time and continued without interruption until the close of early Eocene (Wind River) time. Uplift of all the surrounding mountains and anticlines also took place during this period, but the movements varied in both time and space. By the close of the early Eocene, however, the differential movements between mountains and basins, except those that may be related to sedimentary loading or unloading, had virtually ceased. Thus, for purposes of this report, the term "Laramide" in central Wyoming is applied

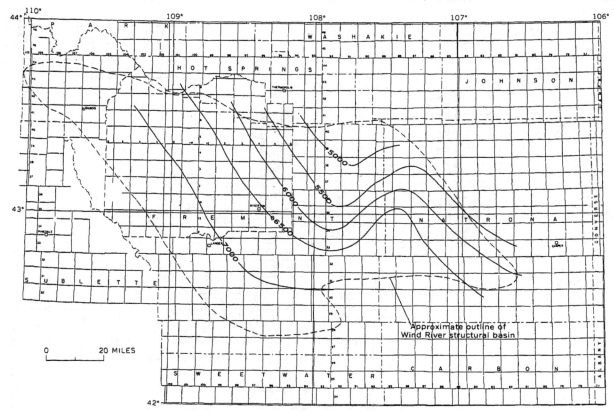

FIGURE 4.—Thickness map of Cody, Mesaverde, Lewis, and Meeteetse Formations (Upper Cretaceous), Wind River Basin. Isopach interval 500 feet. Isopachs are restored across mountain arches where rocks have been eroded.

only to those tectonic events that transpired between the beginning of deposition of the Lance Formation and the end of deposition of the Wind River Formation.

STRUCTURAL GEOLOGY

The Wind River Basin is a broad structural depression bounded by the Wind River Range on the west, the Washakie Range and Owl Creek and southern Bighorn Mountains on the north, the Casper arch on the east, and the Granite Mountains on the south (fig. 1). Along the south and west margins of the basin, Paleozoic and Mesozoic strata dip 10°–20° basinward, whereas along the north and east margins the dips are commonly vertical to overturned. The basin floor is thus markedly asymmetric; the structurally deepest parts are close to the Owl Creek and Bighorn Mountains on the north and to the Casper arch on the east (pls. 2, 3). Southwest asymmetry is a dominant structural characteristic of the region and is exhibited by subsidiary features around the basin margins as well as by all the surrounding mountain uplifts. The northwest structural grain is also conspicuous nearly everywhere (fig. 7).

For convenience, the following discussion is arranged according to major structural provinces or elements within and around the Wind River Basin. Individual features are far too numerous to be described separately; a combination of the geologic map (pl. 1), structure sections (pl. 2), and structure contour map (pl. 3) will suffice to show the essential configuration of most subsidiary folds and faults. The reader is also referred to the original sources of data (inset map, pl. 1) for more detailed information. Many, but not all, structures herein mentioned are labeled on the structure contour map (pl. 3). Many features are also labeled on the structure sections (pl. 2).

MOUNTAIN STRUCTURES

WIND RIVER RANGE

The Wind River Range, culminating in 13,785-foot Gannett Peak, is one of the most extensive mountain uplifts in Wyoming. The range trends northwest along the west side of the Wind River Basin for about 100 miles and has a maximum width of about 50 miles (fig. 1). The broadly exposed Precambrian core is com-

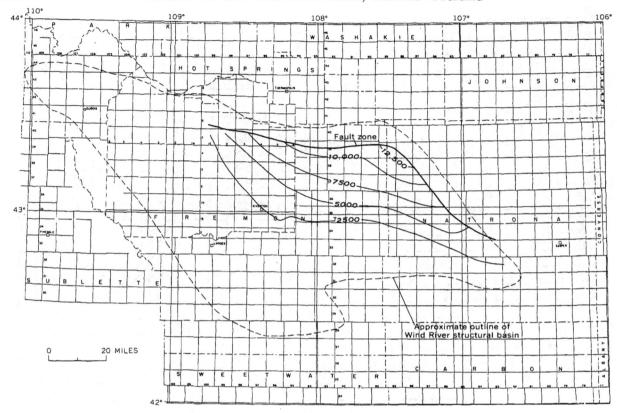

FIGURE 5.—Thickness map of uppermost Cretaceous (Lance Formation) and Paleocene (Fort Union Formation) rocks, Wind River Basin. Isopach interval 2,500 feet.

posed chiefly of gneissic and massive granitic rocks (Parker, 1962, p. 13; Oftedahl, 1953), although layered metasedimentary rocks occur locally, especially at the south end of the range (Bayley, 1965 a–d; Worl, 1963).

The following observations have been made regarding the structure of the Precambrian rocks of the Wind River Range:

1. At the southeast end of the range, tight folds in metasedimentary rocks show a predominant east-northeast trend (Bayley, 1965 a–d), nearly perpendicular to the northwest trend of the present range. Dikes are mostly parallel to the fold axes. A few conspicuous faults trend northwest across the grain of the metasedimentary rocks (Bayley, 1960, p. 222; Worl, 1963, pl. 2).
2. In the central part of the range, west of Lander, conspicuous diabase dikes trend northeast (Parker, 1962, p. 15).
3. At the north end of the range, nearly vertical shear zones are delineated in the Precambrian rocks (Richmond, 1945; Baker, 1946). Nearly all these zones trend north or northwest, and some continue into the flanking sedimentary rocks (Cambrian and younger) as high-angle reverse faults. Worl (1967) mapped several granitic and diabasic dikes, believed to be of Precambrian age, that trend northwest parallel to the most prominent strike of the shear zones; he also distinguished a set of fractures in the Precambrian rocks that trend N. 45° E.

The coverage represented by the foregoing is obviously far too meager to permit even generalized conclusions regarding regional structural trends in the Precambrian rocks of the Wind River Range. It may be surmised, however, that most of the northwest-trending structures are wholly Laramide in origin or that at least the latest movements on them were of Laramide age. East- and northeast-trending structures may represent alinements produced only during Precambrian deformations.

The west flank of the Wind River Range is nearly everywhere overlapped by undeformed Tertiary and Quaternary rocks; an exception is at the northwest corner where steeply dipping Paleozoic and lower Mesozoic strata, and, locally, lower Tertiary rocks, can be seen in fault contact with Precambrian rocks (Richmond, 1945; J. D. Love, written commun., 1966). Seis-

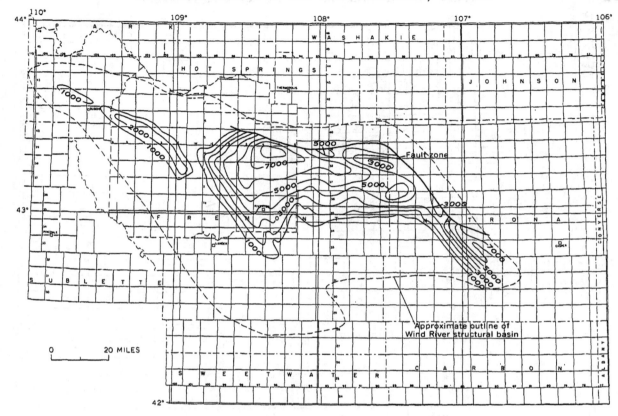

FIGURE 6.—Thickness map of lower Eocene rocks, Wind River Basin. Isopach interval 1,000 feet.

mic and drill data indicate that this entire flank has overridden the east margin of the Green River Basin along thrust faults of great magnitude (Berg, 1961; Berg and Romberg, 1966). Maximum structural relief on the upper surface of the basement complex, between the crest of the range and the trough of the adjacent basin, is probably in excess of 35,000 feet. The major boundary fault (not shown on pl. 1) was called the

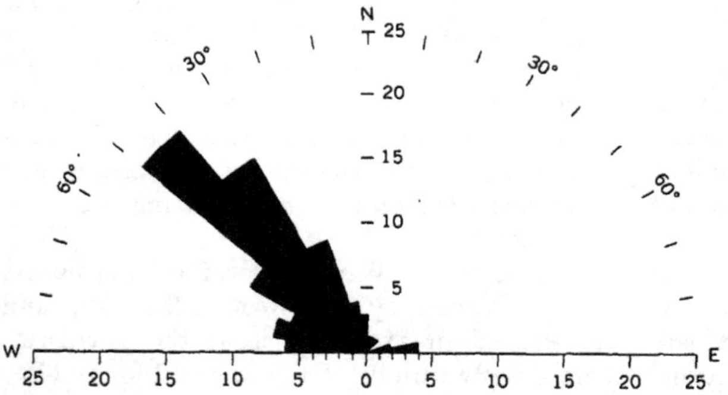

FIGURE 7.—Trends of 92 structural features (anticlines, faults, major synclines) in the Wind River Basin.

Wind River thrust by Richmond (1945); dips range from 30° E. to nearly vertical in the segment exposed at the northwest corner of the range.

A second major fault (also not shown on pl. 1) in the northern part of the range, the White Rock thrust (Richmond, 1945), parallels the Wind River thrust and lies 7-8 miles farther east. Between the two faults, Paleozoic and Mesozoic rocks have been tightly folded in numerous north-trending anticlines and synclines. The dip of the White Rock fault also ranges from 30° E. to nearly vertical. How far the fault extends to the northwest is not known. The northwest end of the Wind River Range is covered by relatively undeformed lower Eocene and younger strata, but detailed mapping in the region by Love and others (1950) and Rohrer (1968) shows that a thick sequence of Paleocene and older rocks along the west flank dip eastward toward the crest where Precambrian rocks are exposed at the highest altitudes (for example, Union Peak). Data from a line of gravity stations across the area, obtained by J. C. Behrendt (oral commun., 1966), indicate a moderate gradient with increasing negative values westward from the crest. The best structural interpretation appears to be that of synclinal folding rather than reverse faulting at the extreme northwest corner of the range (Rohrer, 1968).

Along the east flank of the Wind River Range, Paleozoic and Mesozoic strata form a nearly linear outcrop pattern trending N. 40° W. (pl. 1). These rocks dip uniformly at 12°–15° NE. (basinward) (pl. 2, $A-A'$ to $K-K'$), and descend from the higher parts of the range along a series of prominent dip slopes to the floor of the Wind River Basin (fig. 1). Resistant cherty limestones of the Permian Park City Formation form the outermost series of conspicuous flatirons along the mountain front; less resistant Mesozoic rocks form hogbacks and strike valleys in the lower foothills regions (fig. 8).

The structural continuity of the east flank is interrupted locally by high-angle reverse and normal faults with small stratigraphic displacements and by sharp monoclinal flexures. The flexures, and some faults, trend northwest nearly parallel to the strike of the sedimentary strata, but most of the faults trend east or north, oblique to the strike. At the extreme southeast corner of the range, Bell (1956) mapped two east-northeast-trending faults, which he termed the "Clear Creek and Ellis faults," [2] with apparent left-lateral movement. These two transverse faults are the only major ones in the region; they continue southwestward into Precambrian rocks, and are parallel to structural trends within the latter.

WASHAKIE RANGE

The Washakie Range, at the northwest corner of the Wind River Basin, was named by Love (1939, p. 5), who described it as being a "series of faulted folds, en echelon, beginning with the eastern flank of Black Mountain [NE. cor. T. 6 N., R. 4 W., Wind River Meridian], extending 70 miles northwest of the western end of the Owl Creek Mountains, and ending with the western flank of Buffalo Fork Mountain, west of Togwotee Pass." The eastern two-thirds of the range, as thus defined, lies within the area of the present study.

This uplift, which reaches altitudes of more than 10,000 feet, was completely buried by middle Eocene and younger volcanic rocks of the Absaroka Range, and has now been partly exhumed (fig. 9). Flanking strata of Paleozoic age generally lie at higher altitudes than the Precambrian rocks; this fact is well illustrated by exposures along Horse Creek (fig. 9) and the Wiggins Fork and East Fork Wind Rivers. Love (1939, p. 5) and the present author (Keefer, 1957, p. 205) have expressed the opinion that the still-buried parts of the old Washakie Range are little, if any, higher than the highest altitudes of its presently exposed parts. The central Precambrian core of the range apparently is now visible. The northeast flank remains buried beneath the virtually undeformed pyroclastic rocks of the Absaroka Range.

The larger structural features in the exposed parts of the Washakie Range (pl. 2) are, from west to east, the DuNoir anticline ($A-A'$), Horse Creek and Dubois anticlines ($B-B'$), and East Fork–Black Mountain anticline ($C-C'$, $D-D'$). These folds are strongly asymmetric to the south and southwest, and, although the basinward margins are concealed by Tertiary strata for the most part, each is probably also bounded by a reverse fault (pl. 3).

The Black Mountain fault was mapped by Love (1939, pl. 17) as extending from the southeast corner of Black Mountain (sec. 1, T. 6 N., R. 4 W.) west and northwest about 22 miles to Bear Creek. Farther west, in the Horse Creek drainage, the present author (Keefer, 1957, pl. 26) mapped the EA fault between Horse Creek and Dubois anticlines and extended it eastward along the south edge of Spring Mountain. A well drilled for oil and gas in sec. 9, T. 42 N., R. 105 W. (table 1, well C-2), in the intervening area, encountered a major fault, underlain by Paleozoic and Mesozoic strata, after penetrating nearly 8,000 feet of Precambrian granite. These data suggest strongly that the EA fault, the fault intersected by the well, and the east end of the Black Mountain fault are all segments of a single continuous reverse fault zone extending along the south margin of the Washakie Range for about 25 miles. Such an interpretation is shown on the structure contour map (pl. 3). The northwestern extension of the Black Mountain fault, as mapped by Love, is probably a branching feature, and shows much less displacement than the major fault.

The Washakie Range also includes many subsidiary folds and fault blocks. (For example, see pl. 2, $B-B'$.) Of particular interest are several normal faults, with displacements of as much as 1,000 feet, along the crest of Horse Creek anticline. Considerable normal faulting is also evident at the east end of the East Fork–Black Mountain complex. In the upper Wiggins Fork River drainage, both the Caldwell Meadows and Wiggins Fork Trail reverse faults (pl. 2, $B-B'$) dip westward, and the west blocks are upthrown, which is opposite to the movement of the hanging-wall blocks of most other reverse faults in the region.

Precambrian rocks in the cores of the larger anticlines of the Washakie Range consist chiefly of granite and

---

[2] These faults are largely concealed by Tertiary strata. The Clear Creek fault is shown on pls. 1 and 3, but the Ellis fault is shown only on pl. 1, in the SE. cor. T. 29 N., R. 97 W.

FIGURE 8.—Dip slopes of upper Paleozoic and lower Mesozoic rocks along east flank of Wind River Range; view is northwest along Red Canyon Creek, near southeast corner of range. Table Mountain, composed of horizontal Tertiary strata, forms flat-topped butte on skyline in right center. Arrow is at crest of a small tight anticline. Pp, Park City Formation; ₹r, Triassic rocks; Jr, Jurassic rocks.

FIGURE 9.—Exhumed Paleozoic rocks (Pzr) along Horse Creek, northwestern Wind River Basin. View northward, mainly along crest of Horse Creek anticline in Washaki Range. Horizontal Tertiary volcanic conglomerate and tuff beds (Tv) of Absaroka Range in background. Floor and lower slopes of Horse Creek valley in foreground are composed of Precambrian crystalline rocks mantled by glacial and landslide debris.

granite gneiss (Love, 1939, p. 13-14; Keefer, 1957, p. 163). No detailed study of the basement complex in this range has been attempted.

OWL CREEK MOUNTAINS

The Owl Creek Mountains extend eastward for 75 miles from the east edge of the Absaroka Range to the southwest end of the Bighorn Mountains. The range encompasses a complex group of structures showing diverse trends and tectonic behavior. The unique Wind River Canyon cuts through the central part (fig. 1) and exposes in precipitous canyon walls a complete cross section of one of the major mountain arches of the Rocky Mountains, including the Precambrian core and its detailed relations to the overlying sedimentary rocks (fig. 10). That part of the range lying east of Wind River Canyon has been referred to as the Bridger Range by some previous geologists, but in recent years it has been a more common practice to refer to the entire range as the Owl Creek Mountains.

Structurally, the Owl Creek Mountains can be divided into two distinct parts, separated by Mexican Pass, in the W½ T. 6 N., R. 4 E., which forms a natural dividing line. West of the pass the range is partitioned into several large folds and fault blocks that exhibit a pronounced northwest structural alinement, whereas to the east the structure is virtually that of a single broad east-trending anticlinal arch.

The west half of the Owl Creek Mountains is dominated by a series of rectilinear horsts of Precambrian rocks flanked by lower Paleozoic strata (pl. 2, F-F', G-G'). Individual blocks are almost completely surrounded by reverse faults or sharp monoclinal flexures along which they were differentially uplifted with respect to one another, and also were elevated several thousand feet with respect to the adjacent basins (fig. 11). In gross aspect, the blocks are tilted down toward the northeast, and the most intense deformation occurred around their south and southwest margins. In most areas the structural relations are well exposed and hence readily observed and studied.

The major reverse fault zones are sinuous in outline, some segments trending west and others, northwest. The most extensive fault is the Cottonwood Creek fault (pl. 2, G-G'), which can be traced continuously for 15 miles from the west edge of Jenkins Mountain west and northwest across the entire range. Maximum stratigraphic displacement is about 7,500 feet (Keefer and Troyer, 1964, p. 45-46).

Dips of the faults range from about 30° NE. to nearly vertical. The amount of dip seems to be related to the type of rock present in the footwall blocks, being greatest in resistant rocks (for example, Precambrian rocks faulted against Paleozoic rocks) and least in nonresistant rocks (for example, Precambrian rocks faulted against Upper Cretaceous rocks).

Precambrian rocks in the west half of the Owl Creek Mountains are chiefly granite and granite gneiss cut by conspicuous mafic dikes. The dikes are typically several feet wide and locally are so numerous as to constitute nearly 50 percent of the bedrock. The dikes are alined principally west-northwest, oblique to the pronounced northwest Laramide structural grain but parallel to the more westerly trends of some of the reverse fault segments (Keefer and Troyer, 1964, fig. 13). The latter relationship suggests that the structural pattern in the west half of the range was partly influenced by old lines of weakness in the crystalline basement. The relationships in this part of the range also indicate two distinct

FIGURE 10.—Precambrian (p€g) gneisses, schists, and pegmatite dikes overlain by Cambrian rocks (€r) with depositional contact, Wind River Canyon. Younger Paleozoic rocks form cliffs in background.

FIGURE 11.—Vertical to overturned upper Paleozoic rocks (Pzr) in contact with Triassic rocks (₸r) along south edge of Owl Creek Mountains. Contact is a high-angle reverse fault in places, and numerous faults occur in the Paleozoic sequence farther up draw in center of view. View eastward near Merritt Pass in western part of range. Precambrian rocks (p€) are along crest of major mountain arch, and caprock of Bighorn Dolomite (Ob) dips gently northeastward into Bighorn Basin.

stages of Laramide deformation, both occurring in post-Paleocene pre-early Eocene time. The first stage involved a strong southwest component of movement which produced the conspicuous northwest alinement of structural features. The second stage involved primarily vertical uplift of the various horstlike segments along reverse faults which, in places, cut transversely across the older features. Some of the folds in upper Paleozoic and Mesozoic rocks along the basin margin probably are parts of larger folds that once extended unbroken northwest across the entire mountain range (Keefer and Troyer, 1964, p. 50).

Along the north side of the Owl Creek Mountains, a high-angle reverse fault zone can be traced almost continuously from Mexican Pass west and northwest to Owl Creek Canyon (T. 8 N., R. 2 W.), a distance of about 35 miles. This fault, called the Owl Creek fault by Darton (1906), forms the north boundary of the horsts described above (pl. 2, $F-F'$, $G-G'$). The fault zone dips steeply south and southwest. Stratigraphic displacement is small; Paleozoic rocks are present on both sides in most places.

The junction of the Owl Creek Mountains and the Washakie Range is largely buried by the volcanic rocks of the Absaroka Range. However, similarities in structural development suggest that there is a rather continuous, closely related mountain mass extending about 105 miles from Mexican Pass westward to the west end of the Washakie Range.

The east half of the Owl Creek Mountains, east of Mexican Pass, is a broad east-trending anticlinal complex with a gently dipping (10°–15°) north flank and a steep to overturned south flank. Regional stratigraphic studies and drill data (Keefer, 1965a) indicate that this part of the range has overridden the north margin of the Wind River Basin along a continuous thrust fault zone, here called the South Owl Creek Mountains fault, with as much as 20,000 feet of stratigraphic displacement (pl. 2, $H-H'$, $L-L'$, $M-M'$). Total structural relief on the upper surface of the Precambrian basement, between the crest of the Owl Creek Mountains and the axis of the adjacent Wind River Basin trough, locally exceeds 30,000 feet.

The South Owl Creek Mountains fault is exposed only at its extreme west end along the south edge of Jenkins Mountain (SE. cor. T. 6 N., R. 3 E.) where Jurassic rocks in the hanging-wall (north) block have been placed in contact with Upper Cretaceous rocks in the footwall block. Eastward from Jenkins Mountain the fault is entirely concealed by Eocene strata. However, despite the fact that none of the wells drilled along the north margin of the basin actually penetrates it, the location of the fault can be plotted rather accurately on the basis of data from wells and from detailed mapping of the pre-Eocene rocks along the nearby mountain front.

The dip of the South Owl Creek Mountains fault plane can only be inferred. A well drilled near the west end of the fault zone (table 1, well H-4) bottomed in steeply dipping strata of probable Paleocene age at a depth of 10,000 feet (pl. 2, $H-H'$). The fault was not penetrated by the well; its trace, therefore, must lie a short distance north of the well site. These relations suggest a fault plane that dips steeply northward, perhaps as much as 70°. A regional gravity survey (Case and Keefer, 1966) also suggests a moderately steep dip for the fault all along the south margin of the range (pl. 2, $L-L'$—$N-N'$; fig. 20).

Whether the Owl Creek fault, extending southeast from Mexican Pass, intersects the South Owl Creek Mountains fault is conjectural; the interpretation shown on the structure-contour map (pl. 3) is that they do intersect.

An intricate system of normal faults is present along the south margin of the Owl Creek Mountains in the vicinity of Wind River Canyon (Fanshawe, 1939; Tourtelot and Thompson, 1948; Wise, 1963). These faults are apparently confined to the hanging-wall block of the South Owl Creek Mountains fault; most are alined parallel to the mountain front, but some are transverse to this trend. There is no consistent pattern as to which sides were upthrown or downthrown, but in general, there appears to be a lowering of the marginal part of the range with respect to its crest (Wise, 1963). The most extensive fault is the Boysen fault, which trends nearly east across the canyon from a point 3 miles west of the channel of Wind River to a point 7 miles east (fig. 12). The downdropped block is to the south, and maximum stratigraphic displacement is about 2,000 feet. The normal faults are best explained as having resulted from the tensional fracturing of rigid rocks across the crest of the range as it was being uplifted and arched during Laramide deformation. Individual blocks then collapsed along the steep margin of the range, either at the same time or somewhat later than the arching.

The structurally highest areas in the eastern Owl Creek Mountains lie between Wind River Canyon and the east end of the range. (pl. 2, $M-M'$). Precambrian schist and granite, cut by numerous pegmatite dikes, form the surface rock over much of this region (McLaughlin, 1940; Harley Barnes, U.S. Geological Survey, unpub. map, 1959). The schists strike nearly parallel to the east-west trend of the mountain front and dip steeply (50°–80°) southward. The flanking sedimentary rocks of Cambrian and younger ages along

FIGURE 12.—Exposure of Boysen normal fault (F) in Wind River Canyon, central Owl Creek Mountains. Cambrian rocks (Cr) are faulted down against Precambrian rocks (pC). View is westward across main channel of Wind River. Ob, Bighorn Dolomite; Mm, Madison Limestone.

the south edge of the range, except for a few small erosional windows, are concealed by Eocene strata. These scattered outcrops exhibit fracturing and normal faulting of the flanking strata like that described above for the Wind River Canyon. Possibly some of those occurrences represent ancient landslides that were emplaced during active uplift of the mountains in earliest Eocene time.

The east end of the Owl Creek Mountains plunges 15°–20° eastward and southeastward, and is separated from the Bighorn Mountains by a broad synclinal area (called the Bridger syncline by Tourtelot, 1953) that is largely covered by Eocene strata. Paleozoic and lower Mesozoic strata around the east end of the range are also highly fractured and broken by normal faults with relatively small displacements. The trend of the faults is predominantly east-northeast.

SOUTHERN BIGHORN MOUNTAINS

The southwest end of the Bighorn Mountains forms the northeast margin of the Wind River Basin. Flanking Paleozoic and Mesozoic strata, which dip 15°–25°, wrap around the southwestward-plunging end of the range (Tourtelot, 1953; Woodward, 1957, fig. 2) and are broken by numerous high-angle faults with displacements generally less than 500 feet (pl. 2, O–O', P–P'). The largest feature is the east-northeast-trending Dry Fork fault (pl. 2, P–P'), which can be traced for about 12 miles in intermittent outcrops of upper Paleozoic rocks along Dry Fork of Badwater Creek (Woodward, 1957, fig. 2). The south side, which is upthrown, was assumed by Woodward (p. 243) to be a high-angle reverse fault with a maximum displacement of 300 feet. The southwest end of the Dry Fork fault may intersect the Cedar Ridge normal fault (p. D24), and, like the Cedar Ridge fault, it may have had some post-Laramide movement (Tourtelot, 1953).

The broadly exposed Precambrian core of the southern Bighorn Mountains consists chiefly of highly contorted gneisses and schists cut by numerous irregular pegmatite dikes (Woodward, 1957, p. 215). Specific data regarding structural trends in the basement complex of this region are lacking. However, it is interesting to note that the east-northeast trend of the Dry Fork fault, as well as of several minor faults in this part of the range, is almost precisely parallel with the direction (N. 10°–15° E.) of shear zones in the basement and of major tear faults in flanking sedimentary rocks about 30 miles to the north toward the central part of the range (Hoppin and Palmquist, 1965, p. 997).

Surface mapping and drill data provide ample evidence that the concealed South Owl Creek Mountains fault zone extends eastward from the east end of the Owl Creek Mountains, swings southeast along the southwest edge of the Bighorn Mountains, and continues along the entire west margin of the Casper arch (pl. 3; see, also, discussion of Casper arch below). In the central and northeastern parts of T. 39 N., R. 89 W., outcrops of overturned upper Paleocene strata occur within a mile of southward-dipping Paleozoic rocks at the southwest tip of the Bighorn Mountains (fig. 13; Tourtelot, 1953). The fault passes somewhere between these two series of outcrops and may, in fact, coincide closely with the trace of the Cedar Ridge normal fault. Data from wells drilled a few miles to the south (table 1, wells 0–5, 0–6; pl. 2, *O–O'*), which bottom below 16,500 feet in strata believed to be uppermost Cretaceous (Keefer, 1965a, p. A17), indicate that the stratigraphic displacement on the South Owl Creek Mountains fault here is about 18,000 feet. Farther southeast the actual fault zone was penetrated by a well (table 1, well P–4; pl. 2, *P–P'*) that was drilled about 2 miles south of the mountain front. Relationships in this well suggest that more than one fault may be present in the major zone. Total structural relief on the upper surface of the Precambrian basement, between the crest of the southern Bighorn Mountains and the adjacent Wind River Basin trough, probably exceeds 30,000 feet in places.

CASPER ARCH

The Casper arch is a major, but not deeply eroded, structural upwarp whose steep to overturned west limb forms the east margin of the Wind River Basin. The Upper Cretaceous Cody Shale underlies the broad central part of the arch, and younger Cretaceous and Paleocene strata are exposed in a linear belt all along the west flank (pl. 1). This is a region of low topographic relief, being drained by eastward-flowing tributaries of the Powder and North Platte Rivers which head farther west in the southeastern arm of the Wind River Basin (fig. 1).

A nearly continuous, northwestward-alined series of subsidiary folds occurs along the west edge of the major arch (pl. 3). The largest and structurally highest feature is the Pine Mountain anticline (pl. 2, *S–S'*), which is nearly circular in plan view and which has been breached by erosion to strata as old as Jurassic. Many of these anticlines yield oil and gas.

As noted above, drill data indicate that the South Owl Creek Mountains fault continues all along the west margin of the Casper arch. Three wells in the NE. cor. T. 36 N., R. 87 W., and the SW. cor. T. 37 N., R. 86 W. (table 1, wells Q–6—Q–8; pl. 2, *Q–Q'*), show that the fault dips about 25° NE. and that it has a stratigraphic displacement of about 16,000 feet. Only one fault appears to be present at this locality, but farther southeast, in the SW. cor. T. 35 N., R. 84 W., two more wells (table 1, wells S–2, S–3; pl. 2, *S–S'*) show a highly compressed, imbricated zone. Stratigraphic displacements decrease southeastward, and the fault zone dies out probably in the southwestern part of T. 32 N., R. 82 W. (pl. 2, *T–T'—V–V'*). Maximum structural relief on the upper surface of the Precambrian basement, between the crest of the arch and the adjacent Wind River Basin trough, is about 20,000 feet.

GRANITE MOUNTAINS

The Granite Mountains are unique among mountain ranges in central Wyoming. During Laramide deformation, the range was uplifted several thousand feet with respect to the adjacent basins, and subsequently deeply eroded. Then, owing to a series of extensive downfolding and downfaulting movements, the Precambrian core collapsed and was buried by a thick sequence of middle and upper Tertiary sediments (Love, 1970). At present, the crest of the range is visible only as a series of prominent granite knobs projecting a maximum of 1,000 feet above a nearly level fluvial plain which contains the main channel of the eastward-flowing Sweetwater River (fig. 14). Despite their unique history, however, the Granite Mountains, as a Laramide feature, were similar to the other mountain ranges surrounding the Wind River Basin in structural pattern, tectonic behavior, and relationships to adjacent basin areas.

Precambrian rocks of the Granite Mountains are mainly granite and gneiss cut by scattered mafic dikes. Schist, slate, phyllite, and quartzite are present locally (Love, 1970). Little is known about the detailed lithologies and structural trends of these basement rocks.

Paleozoic and Mesozoic strata, concealed except for a few outcrops, dip uniformly 10°–15° N. off the north flank of the range (pl. 2, *M–M'*, *N–N'*), but they are broken by an extensive system of east-trending normal faults. The fault zone can be traced for about 50 miles, and has been referred to as the North Granite Mountains fault system by Love (1970). The faults originated during the Laramide, at which time the mountain (south) block was upthrown with respect to the south margin of the Wind River Basin (Love, 1970), perhaps locally as much as 5,000 feet. Later, in Pliocene time, the mountain block subsided a few hundred to more than 1,000 feet along virtually the same fault planes. Several large anticlines occur along the north margin of the range (p. D25).

The west and south flanks of the Granite Mountains overrode the southwest margin of the Wind River Basin and the north margin of the Great Divide Basin along the Emigrant Trail thrust fault (Berg, 1961, p. 76) of Laramide origin. This feature is entirely concealed by middle Eocene and younger strata, but its position is well known from drill data (pl. 2, *M–M'*, *N–N'*); it probably extends as far northwest as the west flank of Alkali Butte anticline (pl. 3). Maximum stratigraphic displacement exceeds 20,000 feet (Keefer and Love, 1963, pl. 3), and the plane dips 20° to perhaps as much as 40° NE. Because the core of the Granite

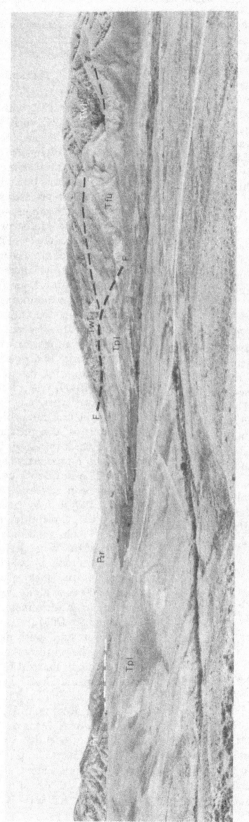

FIGURE 13.—Structural features along Budwater Creek, southwest end of Bighorn Mountains. Along Cedar Ridge normal fault (F), post-lower Eocene rocks (Tpl) are dropped down against vertical to overturned strata of the Paleocene Fort Union Formation (Tfu) and moderately southward dipping strata of the Lysite Member of the lower Wind River Formation (Twl). Buried South Owl Creek Mountains reverse fault occurs between southward-dipping Paleozoic rocks (Pz) of Bighorn Mountains on the left and the Fort Union strata (Tfu) on the right; the fault zone may coincide with the downward projection of the Cedar Ridge normal fault. View is east-southeast.

FIGURE 14.—Bald knobs of granite projecting above level plain of Miocene rocks, central part of Granite Mountains. Notched prominence on right skyline is Split Rock, famous Oregon Trail landmark.

Mountains has been deeply eroded, the total structural relief on the upper surface of the Precambrian basement is uncertain; however, it probably exceeds 30,000 feet with respect to the Great Divide Basin trough along the south edge, and 12,000 feet with respect to the southwestern arm of the Wind River Basin along the west edge.

A broad east-trending syncline developed in the southern part of the Granite Mountains during Miocene and early Pliocene times, and in it was deposited more than 2,000 feet of sediments (Love, 1970). The south edge of this extensive downwarp is bounded by another system of normal faults, called the South Granite Mountains fault system by Love (1970). Along it, the south margin of the range subsided 1,000 feet or more with respect to the adjacent north margin of the Great Divide Basin during early and middle(?) Pliocene time. These movements are largely responsible for the low topographic position of the present crest of the Granite Mountains.

BASIN STRUCTURES

WEST MARGIN

The uniform basinward (northeast) dip of strata off the east flank of the Wind River Range is interrupted by a remarkable series of sharply folded anticlines that stretches from the southwest corner of the Wind River Basin north and northwest to Black Mountain, a distance of nearly 90 miles (pl. 2, $E-E'$ to $M-M'$). Individual folds, from south to north, include the Sweetwater Crossing, Sheep Mountain, Derby, Dallas, Lander-Hudson, Plunkett, Sage Creek, Winkleman, Pilot Butte, Steamboat Butte, Sheldon, Northwest Sheldon, and Dry Creek anticlines (pl. 3). A nearly continuous axis can be drawn, with minor offsets, from Sweetwater Crossing anticline northwest through Winkleman anticline. There, the main trend is offset abruptly 5 miles to the east, and thence continues virtually unbroken almost to Black Mountain. Nearly all the folds show considerable structural closure (500–4,000 ft) in Mesozoic rocks exposed at the surface, and have been the sites of extensive development drilling for oil and gas.

The anticlines are asymmetric to the southwest, and the steep limbs are broken in most places by eastward- and northeastward-dipping reverse faults. South of Winkleman anticline, stratigraphic displacements along the faults probably do not exceed 1,000 feet in most places; but to the north, along the west edge of Pilot Butte, Steamboat Butte, and Dry Creek anticlines, displacements may reach 10,000 feet (pl. 2, $F-F'$). The lower Eocene Wind River Formation appears to be involved in the faulting along the west flanks of Plunkett and Sage Creek anticlines, but not in areas farther north.

The abrupt eastward shift of the anticlinal axis between Winkleman and Pilot Butte may be the result of right-lateral movement along an east-northeast-trending transverse fault. However, there is no positive evidence in drill holes that such a fault exists; so none is shown on the structure-contour map (pl. 3).

Long, narrow synclines lie along the west side of the anticlinal complex, and there is an eastward shift of the main trough line at the northwest end of Winkleman anticline (pl. 3). The syncline southeast of this point is here referred to as the Lander syncline. The syncline to the north was called the North Fork syncline by Love (1939, p. 94), who believed that the axis of the North Fork lay in the central part of the northwestern arm of the Wind River Basin. However, information provided by later drilling (for example, table 1, well C-2) shows that the synclinal axis lies close to, or beneath, the south flank of the Washakie Range (pl. 2, C–C''). Another syncline occurs along the south edges of the Dubois and DuNoir anticlines, in the extreme northwest corner of the basin, but it does not connect with the North Fork syncline (pl. 3).

In the vicinity of the mouth of the East Fork Wind River, lower Eocene and Upper Cretaceous rocks are involved in an imbricate zone of reverse faults (fig. 15). The Wind Ridge fault (pl. 2, C–C', D–D'), can be traced continously for 15 miles parallel to the adjacent front of the Wind River Range. A belt of crumpled Mesozoic rocks lies along the southwest edge of the fault zone. The extent of the faulting at depth is not known, but the faults may pass downward into bedding planes in some of the more incompetent Mesozoic rocks without cutting older strata. This is the largest area in the basin in which lower Eocene rocks are cut by reverse faults.

Near the fault zone just described, large anomalous masses of brecciated Paleozoic rocks are incorporated within lower Eocene strata (Love, 1939, p. 60–61). These masses were probably emplaced as ancient landslides sloughed off during Laramide deformation from the rising East Fork–Black Mountain anticlinal complex.

NORTH MARGIN

Structures along the north margin of the Wind River Basin, west of Mexican Pass, are alternating anticlines and synclines, all with pronounced northwest alinement and southwest asymmetry (pl. 3). Individual features, from east to west, include East Sheep and West Sheep Creeks and Madden, Bargee, and Blacktail anticlines. Nearly all these folds plunge sharply southeastward, and have little, if any, structural closure in surface exposures. Reverse faults are present in places along their southwest limbs. The axes of the intervening synclines converge basinward and plunge eastward and southeastward into the major basin trough area (pl. 3; fig. 16).

Southwest of Blacktail anticline, another conspicuous line of folds, including Circle Ridge (pl. 2, E'–E'), Maverick Springs, and Little Dome (pl. 2, F'–F') anticlines, projects 20 miles southeastward into the basin. The folds are well defined in the flanking Mesozoic strata and show 1,000–2,000 feet of structural closure. Although relationships are obscure in the soft poorly exposed Upper Cretaceous Cody Shale along the steep southwest limbs of the folds, it is probable that this margin of the complex is partly bounded by a northeastward-dipping reverse fault. Data from wells drilled in the northern part of T. 3 N., R. 2 E. (table 1, wells G–1, G–2), indicate that the anticlinal trend continues beneath lower Eocene rocks for at least another 10 miles southeast of Little Dome anticline (pl. 2, G–G'), and that some structural closure is probably present locally along this extension. A subsidiary feature, Merriam anticline, extends 5 miles northeastward from the northeast flank of Little Dome, and is reflected in lower Eocene rocks as well as older strata.

Circle Ridge, Maverick Springs, and Little Dome anticlines are closely related, both structurally and genetically, to the Dry Creek–Northwest Sheldon–Sheldon complex that lies 4–5 miles to the southwest (p. D22).

Structures in pre-lower Eocene rocks along the north

FIGURE 15.—Cretaceous rocks faulted against lower Eocene rocks along north side of Wind River, N.W. cor. T. 5 N., R. 5 W., Wind River meridian. F, Wind Ridge reverse fault; Tle, lower Eocene rocks; Kr, Cretaceous rocks.

FIGURE 16.—Folds in Indian Meadows Formation (lower Eocene) at Shotgun Butte, SE. cor. T. 6 N., R. 1 E., Wind River meridian. Broad syncline through butte is surface expression of major Wind River Basin troughline.

margin of the basin east of Mexican Pass are concealed; thus, they can be interpreted only from seismic and drill data. The dominant feature in this region is the major Wind River Basin trough, whose axis lies 3–15 miles south of the fronts of Owl Creek and Bighorn Mountains (pl. 3). The axis trends east-southeast and appears to intersect the South Owl Creek Mountains fault, at the northwest corner of the Casper arch, almost at a right angle. The structural relations confirm an earlier interpretation, based on regional stratigraphic data by Love, McGrew, and Thomas (1963, fig. 4), that the main trough continued eastward into the Powder River Basin during latest Cretaceous and Paleocene time and was then segmented by the rising Casper arch in early Eocene time.

In the northeast corner of the basin, east of Wind River Canyon, deep drill holes reveal the presence of broad, gentle anticlines between the basin trough and the South Owl Creek Mountains fault zone (pl. 3; pl. 2, $M-M'$, $N-N'$). The meager data suggest that structural closure of 1,000–2,000 feet is present locally and that faulting may also be present in some places. Because these folds occur in some of the structurally deepest areas of the basin, only uppermost Cretaceous and lower Tertiary rocks have been penetrated by wells (max drilling depth, 17,000 ft); older Mesozoic and Paleozoic rocks have not been tested for oil and gas.

Considerable normal faulting occurred in surface rocks of Eocene and younger ages along the north margin of the Wind River Basin. The precise age of the faulting is unknown, but it may have been contemporaneous with similar faulting in the Granite Mountains area, which took place in Pliocene time (Love, 1970). The most extensive feature is the Cedar Ridge normal fault, which can be traced east and southeast for 30 miles from a point about 10 miles east of the Wind River Canyon. The north (mountainward) block is downdropped, and the fault plane may coincide closely with the plane of the buried South Owl Creek Mountains thrust fault (pl. 2, $M-M'$—$O-O'$). Total stratigraphic displacement is unknown; throughout much of its extent, strata of middle(?) and late Eocene age have been dropped against strata of late early Eocene age, a movement of at least a few hundred feet. It seems likely that the plane curves downward into the plane of the South Owl Creek Mountains thrust fault, and that the latest movement along this older fault was therefore in a direction opposite to that of the thrust faulting that had taken place earlier.

A few small folds occur in lower Eocene rocks in the upthrown (basinward) block of the Cedar Ridge normal fault (Tourtelot, 1953). The trends coincide in part with folds in the older rocks at depth, but some of the reversals in dip may also be related to movements along nearby normal faults.

EAST MARGIN

Broad anticlines and synclines characterize the structure along the east margin of the Wind River Basin (pl. 2, Q–Q'—V–V'). The main syncline in this region branches off the major basin trough, near the northwest corner of the Casper arch, and continues southeast along the west flank of the arch (pl. 3). Near the southeast end of the basin, the syncline is split by the West Poison Spider anticline (pl. 2, T–T').

SOUTH MARGIN

Several large anticlinal noses plunge sharply northward and northwestward along the south margin of the Wind River Basin. Many of the trends appear to project far into the interior of the basin, in some places nearly to the center of the major trough area (pl. 3).

The most prominent feature is the Rattlesnake Hills anticline, whose moderately dipping northeast flank forms the west edge of the southeast arm of the basin (pl. 2, P–P'—T–T'). Rocks ranging in age from Precambrian to Paleocene are exposed along this flank, whereas the steep west flank is largely concealed by lower Eocene strata. A reverse fault extends from the center of T. 33 N., R. 88 W., where it is exposed in Paleozoic rocks, probably as far northwest as the center of T. 34 N., R. 89 W.

Numerous igneous plugs (max diameter, 1 mile) and dikes were intruded along the crest of the Rattlesnake Hills and adjacent areas to the southwest. Volcanism occurred largely in middle Eocene time (Carey, 1954b, p. 33), and the now-denuded masses of igneous rocks form the highest peaks in the region (fig. 17). Small-scale folding and faulting of the flanking Paleozoic and lower Mesozoic strata accompanied the intrusions.

West of the Rattlesnake Hills, the larger structural features include Dutton Basin, Muskrat, Conant Creek, Rogers Mountain, and Alkali Butte anticlines (pl. 3). These folds are well defined in strata as young as latest Cretaceous and Paleocene, whereas lower Eocene strata have been involved in the folding only to a minor degree in most places. The anticlines show little, if any, structural closure in surface exposures. However, considerable exploratory drilling, based chiefly on seismic reflectivity data, has been done along the basinward extensions.

Surface mapping and drill data suggest that reverse faults are present along the southwest limbs of all folds, and this interpretation is shown on the structure-contour map (pl. 3). Relationships are obscure in most places, however, owing to poor exposures in Upper Cretaceous shale beds (Cody Shale) and to burial by lower Eocene rocks. The Emigrant Trail reverse fault, the major boundary fault at the west end of the Granite Mountains, probably extends northward along the southwest margins of Rogers Mountain and Alkali Butte anticlines (pl. 2, J–J', K–K'), even though it is nowhere exposed.

Numerous normal faults with small displacements occur along the south margin of the Wind River Basin. They cut strata as young as Miocene and trend parallel to the North Granite Mountains fault system that lies a few miles to the south (pl. 1). Offsets along some of these faults are considered by Zeller (1957, p. 158) to have been a controlling factor in the localization of uranium deposits in lower Eocene rocks in the Gas Hills area. Whether the faults project to sufficient depth to affect all rocks down to, and including, the Precambrian basement, is not known.

FIGURE 17.—Intrusive mass of middle Eocene igneous rocks at Garfield Peak, central Rattlesnake Hills. Dipping strata of Paleozoic and early Mesozoic age surround the intrusion. View is northwest.

West of Rogers Mountain and Alkali Butte anticlines, across the Emigrant Trail fault and an intervening narrow syncline, are two of the largest, and most prolific oil- and gas-producing anticlines in the region, Sand Draw (pl. 2, *K-K'*) and Beaver Creek (pl. 2, *J-J'*). They lie athwart the southwestern arm of the Wind River Basin. Except for small areas of Cody Shale and younger Cretaceous and Paleocene strata along the crest and northeast flank of Sand Draw anticline, the folds are deeply buried and are only slightly reflected in surface exposures of lower Eocene rocks. Numerous drill holes indicate that much minor faulting is present in lower Mesozoic and Paleozoic rocks at depth, and that the southwest flank of Sand Draw anticline is bounded by an eastward-dipping reverse fault (pl. 2, *K-K'*). The folds exhibit 1,000-2,000 feet of structural closure; a small area of independent closure along the northwest extension of the Beaver Creek trend is termed the "Riverton anticline" (pl. 2, *I-I'*).

The main syncline of the southwestern arm of the Wind River Basin continues south and southeast along the west margins of Beaver Creek and Sand Draw anticlines and apparently lies close to, or beneath, the Emigrant Trail thrust fault (pl. 3). Structural relations suggest that this downfold extended into the northern part of the Great Divide Basin as late as early Eocene time, but that it was terminated for the most part along the south edge of the area shown on plate 1 (vicinity of the township corner between Tps. 28 and 29 N., Rs. 94 and 95 W.) by later movements along the South Granite Mountains fault system (Love, 1970).

STRUCTURAL ANALYSIS

FORELAND DEFORMATION

Prucha, Graham, and Nickelsen (1965, p. 966) stated that "Laramide deformation in the central and southern Rocky Mountains east of the folded belts of western Montana and western Wyoming, and east of the Colorado Plateau, is characterized by a structural style which is sufficiently distinctive to merit consideration apart from that of other terrains of the North American Cordillera." The rectilinear, asymmetric anticlinal uplifts and broad, deep synclinal basins of central Wyoming typify the pattern of structures across this ancient foreland region.

One of the most obvious features of foreland deformation in central Wyoming is the close association of the Precambrian basement with the structural development of the entire region. Precambrian crystalline rocks are now widely exposed in the cores of the larger, deeply eroded mountain masses, and deep drill holes in many basin-margin anticlines reveal that the upper surface of the basement is everywhere virtually parallel to the overlying sedimentary units. The relationships leave little doubt that Laramide tectonic stresses acted principally within the basement, and were propagated upward into the younger rocks. The involvement of the basement is perhaps a universal characteristic of foreland structures throughout the world (Lees, 1952, p. 32) and is generally attributed to the fact that relatively thin sedimentary sequences covered those regions at the beginning of deformation. In contrast, structures in mobile belts, which occupy the former sites of miogeosynclines (for example, Overthrust Belt of western Wyoming), commonly represent a shearing-off of sedimentary sequences of great thickness above the basement and a lateral displacement of individual thrust sheets, one upon the other.

The basement complex in central Wyoming was subjected to several episodes of deformation, plutonism, and metamorphism in Precambrian time. The extent to which these inherent lithologic inhomogeneities and structural weaknesses influenced the location and type of structures that developed during Laramide deformation cannot yet be specified. At least a partial control by preexisting zones of weakness in the Precambrian basement is suggested by parallelism of (1) the Clear Creek fault with east-northeast-trending structures in the Precambrian metamorphic rocks at the southeast end of the Wind River Range, (2) granitic and diabasic dikes with northwest-trending shear zones in the Precambrian and flanking sedimentary rocks at the northwest end of the Wind River Range, (3) the east-northeast-trending Dry Fork fault at the south end of the Bighorn Mountains with foliation and shear zones in the basement rocks farther north in the range, and (4) west-northwest-trending Precambrian mafic dikes with high-angle reverse faults in the western Owl Creek Mountains. However, the dominant trend of Laramide structures throughout the region is N. 40° W. (fig. 7), in some places almost normal to the trends of known Precambrian structures. Prucha, Graham, and Nickelsen (1965, p. 989), after a regional investigation of basement control of deformation in the Rocky Mountains, concluded that there is no consistent relation between Laramide structures and basement structures of Precambrian age throughout the region.

MECHANICS OF DEFORMATION

Bucher (1951, p. 517) has stated "One thought runs through all the considerations [of orogenic belts]: Tangential compression dominates the whole record of Earth deformation." Beloussov (1959, p. 3), on the other hand, has proposed that all types of folding originated from the "vertical oscillatory movement of the earth's crust." This question of horizontal versus vertical movements for the origin of Laramide structures in central Wyoming and adjacent regions has been debated by many investigators.[3] The correct interpretation seems to rest ultimately on a knowledge of the behavior and configuration of the major mountain-basin boundary faults at great depth—are the fault planes concave upward (fig. 18A) or concave downward (fig. 18B)? Unfortunately, this important question cannot be answered unequivocally from the data now available.

Observations made during the present study that may be significant to interpretations regarding the nature of Laramide structural movements are summarized in the following paragraphs.

1. *Dips of fault planes.*—The combination of surface and subsurface data indicates that the dips of major reverse faults range from about 25° to nearly vertical; average dips are probably 30°–40°. Horizontal and vertical components of movement for the observed segments of most fault blocks are therefore nearly equal. In general, dips of fault planes appear to be steeper in the resistant Precambrian and Paleozoic rocks than in the less resistant younger rocks. The latter relationship tends to favor the interpretation that mountain-basin boundary faults are concave downward, although the differences in dip may also be related to the differential yielding of various rock types to any given set of tectonic stresses. Dips of fault planes shown on the structure sections, plate 2, are based on an interpretation of all the surface and drill data available in a given area; these dips are projected downward uniformly, and no attempt was made to show either flattening or steepening of the planes at still greater depths.

2. *Structural asymmetry and crustal shortening.*— Marked structural asymmetry, apparent crustal fore-shortening, and the relatively low dips of some thrust faults are features generally attributed to horizontal movement. In gross appearance, all major structural features in central Wyoming seem to have been squeezed and crowded together by strong compressive forces from the north and northeast. Such an interpretation was advocated by Chamberlin (1940), following a synthesis of structural data from the mountain ranges surrounding the Bighorn Basin in north-central Wyoming. Chamberlin reasoned that (a) because of the relatively thin sedimentary cover, the main release of horizontal stresses, acting principally within the basement, was upward, and that (b) because of the lithologic dissimilarities and preexisting lines of weakness in the basement rocks, the region, when compressed, broke into blocks, some parts of which were tilted up to form mountains and some parts tilted down to form basins.

To explain the presence of compressive features along the margins of major uplifts, proponents of the vertical-movement view propose that, as a given uplift forms, vertical movements are transformed to horizontal movements by the gravitational sliding of rock masses off its crest and toward the flanking basins (Beloussov, 1959). The intricate system of normal faults in the vicinity of Wind River Canyon, along the steep south flank of the Owl Creek Mountains, may represent such a phenomenon.

The development of the 90-mile-long series of tightly folded asymmetric anticlines along the gentle east flank of the Wind River Range, how-

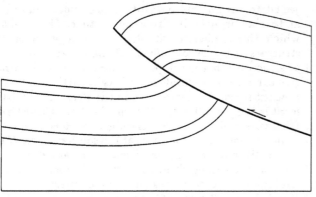

A. Lateral compression

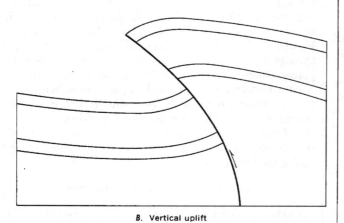

B. Vertical uplift

FIGURE 18.—Alternate interpretations regarding crustal movement in central Wyoming.

---

[3] See Fanshawe (1939), Chamberlin (1940), Berg (1961), and Blackstone (1963, p. 177–178) for discussions of the horizontal-movement view, and Osterwald (1961), Eardley (1963), Wise (1963), and Prucha, Graham, and Nickelsen (1965) for discussions of the vertical-movement view.

ever, is more difficult to interpret in terms of horizontal movements induced by vertical uplift of the nearby mountain mass—in this case, overturning and reverse faulting is toward the uplift rather than away from it. Similar features also occur along the gentle flanks of mountain ranges surrounding the Bighorn Basin (Chamberlin, 1940). The origin of these structures seems best explained by regional compressive forces (actually from the basinward side) that are unrelated to vertical uplift.

3. *Relation of folding to faulting.*—Displacements in a vertical stress system are generally considered to be accomplished primarily by faulting and only to a lesser degree by folding (for example, see Sanford, 1959, fig. 18; Billings, 1960, fig. 16; Prucha and others, 1965, fig. 23). In this interpretation the basement complex is assumed to be a rigid mass incapable of large-scale flexing; as deformation begins, the basement yields primarily by faulting, and the resulting offset is reflected initially by monoclinal folds in the overlying sedimentary rocks and finally by rupture. In central Wyoming, however, the evidence heavily favors the interpretation that faulting developed as a consequence of folding. Uplifts began as relatively simple symmetrical folds, which then became progressively more asymmetrical as movement intensified, and finally ruptured along the attenuated limb of the steep side (Berg, 1961, p. 79; Keefer and Love, 1963, pl. 4). The latter pattern seems most easily obtained by lateral stresses.

4. *Basin subsidence.*—The Wind River Basin and other basins subsided as the mountains rose throughout the Laramide deformational period. In large segments of some basins, subsidence was equal to, or exceeded, the amount of uplift of the adjacent mountains. Furthermore, downwarping apparently began in some places before the mountains started to rise (Keefer and Love, 1963; Love, McGrew, and Thomas, 1963), which seems to answer satisfactorily the long-debated question of whether subsidence is a consequence of sedimentary loading, or vice versa.

Many authors have pointed out that sedimentary loading alone cannot account for all the observed subsidence. The basin-fill sediments are less dense (less than 2.4 g per cc) than the underlying materials which they are depressing (greater than 2.67 g per cc); thus, without an additional process operating to pull it down, the basin would eventually fill up to the base level of deposition, and subsidence would cease. It might be argued that, if the mountains rose faster than the basin subsided, the rate of erosion would increase proportionally and provide enough clastic material to the basin area to sustain subsidence. In the Wind River Basin, however, the base level of deposition remained virtually at sea level throughout Late Cretaceous and early Tertiary times and did not start to rise until the end of early Eocene time. It is therefore concluded that subsidence kept pace with sedimentation only because forces other than sedimentary loading pulled the basin down. The amount of downfolding (max 17,000 ft) is difficult to explain solely in terms of horizontal compression without supplementation by vertically oriented forces.

The foregoing discussion indicates that certain characteristics of Laramide structural features in central Wyoming favor the vertical-movement explanation, whereas other characteristics favor the horizontal-movement explanation. The fact that the evidence is contradictory probably indicates that no single stress system can be applied uniformly to all parts of the region, or to all stages of the orogeny. An excellent case in point occurs in the western part of the Owl Creek Mountains. There, the greatest amount of deformation took place between the deposition of the Fort Union (Paleocene) and Indian Meadows (earliest Eocene) Formations, but it was accomplished during two distinct stages (Keefer and Troyer, 1964, p. 50). During the first stage the region was subjected to a strong horizontal component of movement from the northeast, resulting in an extensive series of parallel folds, all asymmetric and faulted toward the southwest. During the second stage, movement was largely vertical along high-angle reverse faults that dip mountainward on both sides of the uplift; in some places these faults clearly cut across the trend of the earlier fold system (pl. 1). Thus, the Precambrian core of the western Owl Creek Mountains appears as a series of upraised wedges with respect to the adjacent basin areas (pl. 2, $F-F'$, $G-G'$). Whether the upward movement of the wedges was the culmination of yielding to horizontal stresses or was caused by direct vertical pressure is indeterminable. It is interesting to note that, during the late stages of the Laramide, high-angle faults also developed on the north margin of the Granite Mountains, along which the mountain block was upthrown (Love, 1970), that faulting and sharp monoclinal folding occurred in places along the northeast flank of the Wind River Range (pl. 2, $C-C'$) and that southwestward-dipping reverse faults developed along the northeast margins of some of the folds in the Washakie Range (pl. 2, $B-B'$). The features along the gentle flanks of the mountains, however, are small compared with those along the steep flanks.

A third possible explanation for the origin of Laramide structures in central Wyoming, and one that has not received much attention from structural geologists in the past, is that of strike-slip or transcurrent faulting. Large-scale lineaments or faults, transverse to major Laramide trends, have been described in southeastern Wyoming (Blackstone, 1951, p. 27), in the Bighorn Mountains (Chamberlin, 1940, p. 684–687) and in south-central Montana (Osterwald, 1961, fig. 7). It is probable that appreciable strike-slip movements occurred along some of these features and that they exerted a significant influence on regional structural patterns.

The east and west borders of the Wind River Basin trend N. 40° W., and the north and south borders trend nearly due east (pl. 1). Perhaps this parallelogram is due to left-lateral shear—the Granite Mountains having moved relatively eastward along the south edge of the basin, and the Owl Creek Mountains having moved relatively westward along the north edge. En echelon northwest-trending faults and folds along both these margins could be attributed to such a rotational stress system (Mead, 1920, fig. 12; Campbell, 1958, fig. 1).

Although east-west fault zones occur along the south flank of the Owl Creek Mountains and along the north flank of the Granite Mountains, no appreciable strike-slip movements can be demonstrated on the basis of present data. Bell (1956) has described strike-slip movements along east-northeast-trending faults at the south end of the Wind River Range, but there is no evidence that this trend continues eastward across the southwestern arm of the Wind River Basin and connects with the North Granite Mountains fault system (pl. 3).

Deformation in late Tertiary time was dominated by vertical movements along normal faults which coincide in part with the older Laramide reverse fault zones. In general, the normal faulting resulted in a lowering of the mountain masses with respect to the basin.

REGIONAL UPLIFT

Stratigraphic and structural relations throughout central Wyoming and adjacent regions show that the basins were once filled with thick sequences of post-lower Eocene rocks that buried all but the highest mountain ridges. These rocks have now been almost completely removed by erosion. Original thicknesses are unknown, but fairly reliable estimates can be made in the Wind River Basin by drawing a line from the high plateau surface of the Absaroka Range (alt 11,000 ft) southeastward to Beaver Divide (alt 7,000 ft). These two areas represent the erosional remnants of post-lower Eocene rocks along the northwest and south edges of the basin, respectively (pl. 1). On this basis, assuming a uniform gradient between the two outcrops, the thickness of Tertiary rocks stripped out of the central part of the basin was about 3,000 feet.

Although the evidence is circumstantial, there is general agreement that this cycle of degradation (which is still continuing), as well as the high average elevation of the present-day landscape, was initiated by uniform regional uplift that caused a widespread change in base level sometime during the late Tertiary. The concept was discussed in an early study of the region by Blackwelder (1915, p. 193–210), and later investigations have strengthened the hypothesis. No other reasonable explanation has yet been given to account for all the observed relationships.

Blackwelder's interpretations were based primarily on the presence of conspicuous concordant erosional surfaces at altitudes of 11,000–12,000 feet above sea level in the Wind River Range. He believed that these surfaces represented an episode of regional planation (largely by stream abrasion) that took place at considerably lower altitudes than the present, probably during late Miocene and Pliocene time (Blackwelder, 1915, p. 210). The implication is that the surfaces were cut during the maximum stage of sedimentary filling of the adjacent basins (for example, see Love, 1960, p. 212), when the master drainage systems were virtually at grade.

One of the most convincing arguments for regional uplift is provided by stratigraphic and paleontologic data from lower Tertiary rocks in the Wind River Basin. Sedimentary features and fossil floras and faunas in these strata indicate that a warm-temperate to subtropical climate characterized most of Paleocene and Eocene time (Dorf, 1960). It is therefore inferred that basin subsidence kept pace with sedimentation and that the base level of deposition was never far above sea level during these epochs. Under these conditions, the altitude of the central part of the basin is arbitrarily placed at 1,500 feet or less above sea level at the end of the early Eocene (fig. 21). In contrast, uppermost lower Eocene strata now occur at an altitude of 6,500 feet near Beaver Divide, and at even higher altitudes in the northwestern part of the basin. Assuming that sea level has remained relatively constant, the above relationships suggest that the basin floor has been elevated about 5,000 feet since the deposition of the lower Eocene rocks. It appears that the uplift affected mountains and basin to the same degree in those areas where the lower Eocene rocks still lap onto the adjacent mountain flanks with little basinward dip. Exceptions to this are along the south edge of the Owl Creek Mountains and along both

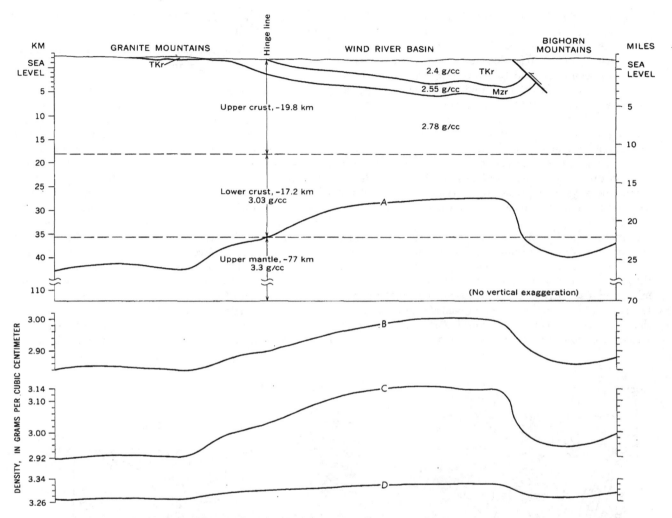

FIGURE 19.—Possible variations in density and crustal thickness required for present crustal equilibrium in the Wind River Basin and adjacent mountain ranges. Crustal model at basin hinge line assumed to be the same as that at Flaming Gorge, Utah (Jackson and Pakiser, 1965). Line of section shown in figure 20. A, Position of Mohorovicic discontinuity if all densities remain constant; B, Required variations in density of total crust below top of Paleozoic rocks if all other densities remain constant and surfaces of discontinuity remain horizontal; C, Required variations in density of lower crust if all other densities remain constant and surfaces of discontinuity remain horizontal; D, Required variations in density of upper mantle if all other densities remain constant and surfaces of discontinuity remain horizontal; TKr, Tertiary and uppermost Cretaceous rocks; Mzr, older Mesozoic rocks.

margins of the Granite Mountains, where the mountain masses were lowered a few hundred to a few thousand feet with respect to the basin on normal faults that were probably activated during the uplift.

Love (1970) presents evidence from the Granite Mountains area that the greatest part of the uplift probably occurred during Pliocene time.

The concept of uniform regional uplift has also been used to explain similar phenomena in many other parts of the Rocky Mountains. Both the age and the estimated magnitude of the uplift in central Wyoming agree well with interpretations made by Gilluly (1963, p. 155) regarding the uplift of the Colorado Plateau, although Hunt (1956, p. 77) believed that the latter feature had begun to rise as early as Miocene time.

VOLCANISM

Extensive eruptions in the Absaroka-Yellowstone volcanic field of northwestern Wyoming during middle Eocene and later Tertiary times were undoubtedly closely related to geologic events in the surrounding regions. Possible areas from which such tremendous volumes of material were withdrawn from the subsurface include the nearby intermontane basins of Laramide origin. In the Wind River Basin, however, Laramide deformation had virtually ceased by middle Eocene time; so there is considerable doubt that any significant part of the downwarping resulted from the volcanic activity. There is a possibility, on the other hand, that basin subsidence was one of the underlying causes for volcanism. Late in early Eocene time parts of the basin floor had been depressed 15,000 feet or more below their previous level. At this stage of basin development, the increase in temperature in deep zones of the crust or upper mantle may have been sufficient to induce partial melting of materials that eventually could have migrated into the Absaroka-Yellowstone volcanic region. If this were indeed true, eruptions might be expected to have occurred at other localities in the Wind River Basin and adjacent uplifts. None are present, except for small intrusions of middle Eocene age in the Rattlesnake Hills.

A more logical approach may be to relate the volcanic activity to post-Laramide deformation. Blackstone (1951, p. 28), for example, has expressed the opinion that the late Tertiary normal faulting in central Wyoming and elsewhere is a direct consequence of the transfer of subcrustal materials from beneath these areas to the sites of eruption. Considerable downwarping of areas closer to the volcanic field, such as Jackson Hole (Love, 1956, p. 148), also occurred in late Tertiary (middle Pliocene) time.

CRUSTAL STRUCTURE AND THE IMPLICATIONS OF ISOSTASY

Laramide deformation resulted in displacements of 30,000–35,000 feet, which represents more than one-quarter of the estimated total thickness of the crust now present in central Wyoming. Such pronounced offsets could only accompany widespread adjustments in the deeper zones of the crust and upper mantle. It has therefore been proposed that "All major topographic deviations above and below sea level can persist only when they are isostatically compensated; this certainly applies to deviations equivalent in size to blocks 100 km × 100 km, and probably to any block 20 km × 20 km" (Sitter, 1956, p. 333). Strong supporting evidence for this view is the well-established fact that even small parts of the crust subsided beneath icecaps or bodies of water and rebounded after the ice or water was removed (for example, see Crittenden, 1963).

A crustal model from the Flaming Gorge area in southwestern Wyoming and northeastern Utah is used

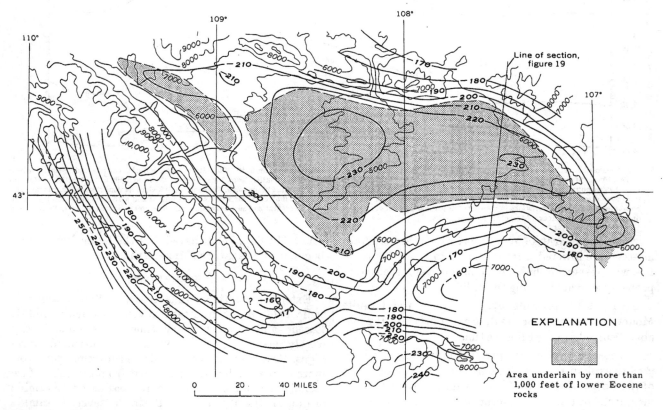

FIGURE 20.—Map showing relations of Bouguer gravity anomalies (interval 10 mgals) to regional topography (contour interval 1,000 ft) and areas of thickest sequences of low-density sedimentary rocks in the Wind River Basin and surrounding mountain ranges. Gravity data from Case and Keefer (1966) and Berg and Romberg (1966).

as a guide in applying the principles of isostasy to crustal structure in the Wind River Basin and surrounding uplifts. In that model the thicknesses of the crust and upper mantle, as computed from geophysical data, are 37 km and 77 km, respectively (Willden, 1965, table 2; Jackson and Pakiser, 1965, fig. 7). The assumption is made, therefore, that all compensations take place above the 114-km level. Density values are assigned as follows: Lower Tertiary and uppermost Cretaceous rocks, 2.4 g/cc; older Mesozoic rocks, 2.55 g/cc; Paleozoic strata and basement rocks of the upper crust, 2.78 g/cc (average to depth of 19.8 km); lower crustal materials, 3.03 g/cc; upper mantle materials, 3.3 g/cc. The values for materials below the top of the Paleozoic sequence are based on velocities as determined from seismic-refraction records by Jackson and Pakiser (1965, fig. 7). The values for the post-Paleozoic rocks, though not based on direct measurements of density throughout the column (such data are very meager), seem to be geologically plausible, and they fit within the ranges generally assigned to them (for example, see Berg and Romberg, 1966, p. 649; Case and Keefer, 1966).

Figure 19 illustrates some hypothetical two-dimensional combinations of thicknesses and densities that would produce isostatic equilibrium at present. The structure section is simplified from section O–O' (pl. 2), as extended southward to include the central Granite Mountains. The crustal model from the Flaming Gorge area described in the preceding paragraph is plotted at the "hinge-line" between the Granite Mountains and Wind River Basin, a position that was arbitrarily chosen to represent the average set of conditions existing in the region at present. To maintain equilibrium, the rock columns underlying the mountain provinces must have a lower average density than do those beneath the basin. Either the crust is thicker, or the crust and (or) mantle is less dense, beneath the mountains. The condition for true isostatic compensation, however, is probably not shown by any single one of the idealized curves in figure 19, but is most likely represented by some combination of all the factors involved (Pakiser and Steinhart, 1964, p. 145).

Attempts to evaluate the actual status of isostasy in the region have been made from gravity data. These data show that anomalies are closely related to (1) regional topography, (2) areas of greatest thicknesses of low-density sedimentary rocks, and (3) elevation and structural configuration of the upper surface of the Precambrian basement (fig. 20). Thus, the mountain provinces exhibit relative positive anomalies (max. about −160 mgals) with respect to the basin provinces (min about −280 mgals). Observed gravity values across the Uinta and Wind River Ranges, however, are interpreted by Behrendt and Thiel (1963), and Berg and Romberg (1966), respectively, to be too large for the densities normally assigned to the basement rocks in these areas. They conclude that denser rocks (for example, basalt) must lie at shallower depths beneath the mountains than they do beneath the basins, and, consequently, that local isostatic adjustment has not been achieved. The fact that some mountain blocks collapsed and (or) that some segments of the basin floor rebounded along normal faults in late Tertiary time may likewise be interpreted to indicate that local imbalances existed after the close of the Laramide. The absence of severe or frequent earthquakes in the region during modern times, on the other hand, suggests a state of current crustal stability.

Comparisons were made, during the present study, of the amounts of Laramide uplift and subsidence, considering only that region that stretches from mountain crest to mountain crest [4] on opposite sides of the Wind River Basin. Calculations were based on three-dimensional data obtained from the cross-sectional areas shown on the structure sections (pl. 2) and the distances between individual sections (pl. 1). Measurements were made on top of the Precambrian basement, and represent the difference in elevations of that surface from its position at the beginning of deformation (latest Cretaceous time) to its position at the end of deformation (end of early Eocene time). Fairly reliable restorations of the basement surface can be made for these periods, based on the present structural configuration of the region and on the assumptions that (1) sea level remained constant during deformation, (2) the base level of deposition across the central part of the basin did not exceed an average elevation of 1,500 feet above sea level at the close of early Eocene time, and (3) post-Laramide differential movements between mountains and basin were negligible (for the order of magnitude involved in the computations), except in the Granite Mountains area where necessary considerations were made of late Tertiary normal faulting. The methods used are shown graphically in figure 21.

The calculations show that the ratio of uplift to subsidence during the Laramide was more than 2.5:1; about 14,500 cubic miles of basement rock went up and about 5,500 cubic miles went down. If these differential movements were averaged, the net result would be a rise in elevation of the upper surface of the Precambrian basement across the entire region of about 4,500 feet. This is not to be construed as the rise in elevation of the actual ground surface, however; erosion of the

---

[4] Present-day mountain crests are assumed to correspond closely to the Laramide structural crests. Parts of mountain ranges that fall outside this perimeter should be considered in similar comparisons of uplift and subsidence for the next adjacent basins.

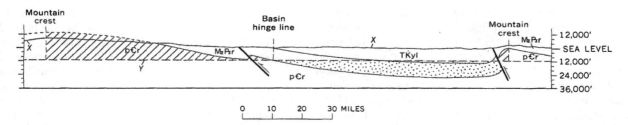

FIGURE 21.—Diagrammatic cross section showing method used in calculating amounts of Laramide uplift and subsidence. X, Topographic surface at end of deformation in early Eocene time; Y, Position of top of Precambrian basement at beginning of deformation in Late Cretaceous time. Subsided area is stippled; uplifted areas are ruled and include only areas that lie on the Wind River Basin side of the mountain crests. TKyl, Lance Formation and younger rocks; Mz Pzr, pre-Lance sedimentary rocks; pCr, Precambrian rocks.

mountain masses and aggradation in the basin area would have limited the average rise of the ground surface to perhaps 3,000 feet. The ratio of the amount of rock eroded to the amount of sediments deposited during the orogeny is calculated to be about 2 to 1 (13,000 versus 6,500 cubic miles). Although sediments continued to accumulate in the basin and along the adjacent mountain flanks from middle Eocene through early Pliocene times, these were largely of volcanic origin and not locally derived. Furthermore, the effects of the additional loading on regional crustal structure would have been nearly balanced by the subsequent removal of the sediments by erosion from much of the basin area.

Similar considerations of volumes are necessary for all the adjacent basins and mountains in Wyoming before the significance of the figures given above can be evaluated. However, if the relationships in the area of the present study are representative, then it is evident that (1) the uplifts were not compensated statically merely by material flowing laterally from beneath the basin or by sedimentary loading; and (2) to achieve equilibrium, either the crust was thickened beneath the mountains by the addition of enormous quantities of materials of crustal density, or else the density of the upper mantle was decreased. The actual conditions can be determined only through a more fundamental knowledge of the physical and chemical properties of crust and mantle materials.

REFERENCES CITED

Andrews, D. A., 1944, Geologic and structure contour map of the Maverick Springs area, Fremont County, Wyoming: U.S. Geol. Survey Oil and Gas Inv. Prelim. Map 13.

Armstrong, F. C., and Oriel, S. S., 1965, Tectonic development of Idaho-Wyoming thrust belt: Am. Assoc. Petroleum Geologists Bull., v. 49, no. 11, p. 1847–1866.

Baker, C. L., 1946, Geology of the northwestern Wind River Mountains, Wyoming: Geol. Soc. America Bull., v. 57, no. 6, p. 565–596.

Bayley, R. W., 1960, Precambrian taconite deposits near Atlantic City, Fremont County, Wyoming, in Overthrust belt of southwestern Wyoming and adjacent areas: Wyoming Geol. Assoc. Guidebook 15th Ann. Field Conf., 1960, p. 222–225.

——— 1965a, Geologic map of the South Pass City quadrangle, Fremont County, Wyoming: U.S. Geol. Survey Geol. Quad. Map GQ–458.

——— 1965b, Geologic map of the Atlantic City quadrangle, Fremont County, Wyoming: U.S. Geol. Survey Geol. Quad. Map GQ–459.

——— 1965c, Geologic map of the Miners Delight quadrangle, Fremont County, Wyoming: U.S. Geol. Survey Geol. Quad. Map GQ–460.

——— 1965d, Geologic map of the Louis Lake quadrangle, Fremont County, Wyoming: U.S. Geol. Survey Geol. Quad. Map GQ–461.

Behrendt, J. C., and Thiel, E., 1963, A gravity and magnetic survey of the Uinta Mountains: Jour. Geophys. Research, v. 68, no. 3, p. 857–868.

Bell, W. G., 1955, The geology of the southeastern flank of the Wind River Mountains, Fremont County, Wyoming: Wyoming Univ. unpub. Ph. D. dissert., 204 p.

——— 1956, Tectonic setting of Happy Springs and nearby structures in the Sweetwater uplift area, central Wyoming, in Am. Assoc. Petroleum Geologists Rocky Mtn. Sec. Geol. Rec.: p. 81–86.

Beloussov, V. V., 1959, Types of folding and their origin: Internat. Geology Rev., v. 1, no. 2, p. 1–21.

Berg, R. R., 1961, Laramide tectonics of the Wind River Mountains, in Wyoming Geol. Assoc. Guidebook 16th Ann. Field Conf., 1961: p. 70–80.

Berg, R. R., and Romberg, F. E., 1966, Gravity profile across the Wind River Mountains, Wyoming: Geol. Soc. America Bull., v. 77, no. 6, p. 647–655.

Billings, M. P., 1960, Diastrophism and mountain building: Geol. Soc. America Bull., v. 71, no. 4, p. 363–397.

Blackstone, D. L., Jr., 1951, An essay on the development of structural geology in Wyoming, in Wyoming Geol. Assoc. Guidebook 6th Ann. Field Conf., 1951: p. 15–28.

——— 1963, Development of geologic structure in central Rocky Mountains, in The backbone of the Americas—Tectonic history from pole to pole: Am. Assoc. Petroleum Geologists Mem. 2, p. 160–179.

Blackwelder, Eliot, 1915, Post-Cretaceous history of the mountains of central western Wyoming: Jour. Geology, v. 23, p. 97–117, 193–217, 307–340.

Bucher, W. H., 1951, Fundamental properties of orogenic belts, in Gutenberg, Beno, chm., Colloquium on plastic flow and deformation within the earth: Am. Geophys. Union Trans., v. 32, no. 4, p. 514–517.

Campbell, J. D., 1958, En echelon folding: Econ. Geology, v. 53, no. 4, p. 448–472.

Carey, B. D., Jr., 1954a, Geologic map and structure sections of the Rattlesnake Hills Tertiary volcanic field, Natrona County, Wyoming, in Wyoming Geol. Assoc. Guidebook 9th Ann. Field Conf., 1954 [map in pocket].

———1954b, A brief sketch of the geology of the Rattlesnake Hills, in Wyoming Geol. Assoc. Guidebook 9th Ann. Field Conf., 1954: p. 32–34.

Case, J. E., and Keefer, W. R., 1966, Regional gravity survey, Wind River Basin, Wyoming, in Geological Survey research 1966: U.S. Geol. Survey Prof. Paper 550–C, p. C120–C128.

Chamberlin, R. T., 1940, Diastrophic behavior around the Bighorn basin [Mont.-Wyo.]: Jour. Geology, v. 48, no. 7, p. 673–716.

Crittenden, M. D., Jr., 1963, Effective viscosity of the Earth derived from isostatic loading of Pleistocene Lake Bonneville: Jour. Geophys. Research, v. 68, no. 19, p. 5517–5530.

Darton, N. H., 1906, Geology of the Owl Creek Mountains: U.S. 59th Cong., 1st sess., S. Doc. 219, 48 p.

Dorf, Erling, 1960, Climatic changes of the past and present: Am. Scientist, v. 48, no. 3, p. 341–364.

Dunnewald, J. B., 1958, Geology of the Fish Lake Mountain area, Fremont County, Wyoming: Wyoming Univ. unpub. master's thesis.

Eardley, A. J., 1963, Relation of uplifts to thrusts in Rocky Mountains, in The backbone of the Americas—Tectonic history from pole to pole: Am. Assoc. Petroleum Geologists Mem. 2, p. 209–219.

Fanshawe, J. R., 1939, Structural geology of the Wind River Canyon area, Wyoming: Am. Assoc. Petroleum Geologists Bull., v. 23, no. 10, p. 1439–1492.

Flanagan, P. E., 1955, Geology of the Mud Creek area, Hot Springs County, Wyoming: Wyoming Univ. unpub. master's thesis, 57 p.

Gilliland, J. D., 1959, Geology of the Whisky Mountain area, Fremont County, Wyoming: Wyoming Univ. unpub. master's thesis.

Gilluly, James, 1963, The tectonic evolution of the western United States: Geol. Soc. London Quart. Jour., v. 119, no. 2, p. 133–174.

Gooldy, P. L., 1948, Beaver Creek-South Sheep Mountain area [Wyoming, geol. map], in Wyoming Geol. Assoc. Guidebook 3d Ann. Field Conf., Wind River Basin, 1948 [map in pocket].

Hares, C. J., 1946, Geologic map of the southeastern part of the Wind River Basin and adjacent areas in central Wyoming: U.S. Geol. Survey Oil and Gas Inv. Prelim. Map. 51.

Hoppin, R. A., and Palmquist, J. C., 1965, Basement influence on later deformation, the problem, techniques of investigation, and examples from Bighorn Mountains, Wyoming: Am. Assoc. Petroleum Geologists Bull., v. 49, no. 7, p. 993–1003.

Hunt, C. B., 1956, Cenozoic geology of the Colorado Plateau: U.S. Geol. Survey Prof. Paper 279, 99 p.

Jackson, W. H., and Pakiser, L. C., 1965, Seismic study of crustal structure in the Southern Rocky Mountains, in Geological Survey research 1965: U.S. Geol. Survey Prof. Paper 525–D, p. D85–D92.

Keefer, W. R., 1957, Geology of the Du Noir area, Fremont County, Wyoming: U.S. Geol. Survey Prof. Paper 294–E, p. 155–221.

———1965a, Stratigraphy and geologic history of the uppermost Cretaceous, Paleocene, and lower Eocene rocks in the Wind River Basin, Wyoming: U.S. Geol. Survey Prof. Paper 495–A, p. A1–A77.

———1965b, Geologic history of Wind River Basin, central Wyoming: Am. Assoc. Petroleum Geologists Bull., v. 49, no. 11, p. 1878–1892.

Keefer, W. R., and Love, J. D., 1963, Laramide vertical movements in central Wyoming: Wyoming Univ. Contr. Geology, v. 2, no. 1, p. 47–54.

Keefer, W. R., and Rich, E. I., 1957, Stratigraphy of the Cody shale and younger Cretaceous and Paleocene rocks in the western and southern parts of the Wind River Basin, Wyoming, in Wyoming Geol. Assoc. Guidebook 12th Ann. Field Conf., Southwest Wind River Basin, 1957: p. 71–78.

Keefer, W. R., and Troyer, M. L., 1964, Geology of the Shotgun Butte area, Fremont County, Wyoming: U.S. Geol. Survey Bull. 1157, 123 p.

Keefer, W. R., and Van Lieu, J. A., 1966, Paleozoic formations in the Wind River Basin, Wyoming: U.S. Geol. Survey Prof. Paper 495–B, p. B1–B60.

Ketner, K. B., Keefer, W. R., Fisher, F. S., Smith, D. L., and Raabe, R. G., 1966, Mineral resources of the Stratified Primitive Area, Wyoming: U. S. Geol. Survey Bull. 1230–E, p. E1–E56.

Kisling, D. C., 1962, Geology of the Antelope Ridge area, Fremont and Hot Springs Counties, Wyoming: Wyoming Univ. unpub. master's thesis.

Lees, G. M., 1952, Foreland folding: Geol. Soc. London Quart. Jour., v. 108, p. 1–34.

Long, J. S., Jr., 1959, Geology of the Phlox Mountain area, Hot Springs and Fremont Counties, Wyoming: Wyoming Univ. unpub. Master's thesis, 185 p.

Love, J. D., 1939, Geology along the southern margin of the Absaroka Range, Wyoming: Geol. Soc. America Spec. Paper 20, 134 p.

———1956, Summary of geologic history of Teton County, Wyoming, during Late Cretaceous, Tertiary, and Quaternary times, in Wyoming Geol. Assoc. Guidebook 11th Ann. Field Conf., Jackson Hole, 1956: p. 140–150.

———1960, Cenozoic sedimentation and crustal movement in Wyoming (Bradley volume): Am. Jour. Sci., v. 258–A, p. 204–214.

———1970, Cenozoic geology of the Granite Mountains area, central Wyoming: U.S. Geol. Survey Prof. Paper 495–C (in press).

Love, J. D., Johnson, C. O., Nace, H. L., and others, 1945, Stratigraphic sections and thickness maps of Triassic rocks in central Wyoming: U.S. Geol. Survey Oil and Gas Inv. Prelim. Chart 17.

Love, J. D., McGrew, P. O., and Thomas, H. D., 1963, Relationship of latest Cretaceous and Tertiary deposition and deformation to oil and gas in Wyoming, in The backbone of the Americas—Tectonic history from pole to pole: Am. Assoc. Petroleum Geologists Mem. 2, p. 196–208.

Love, J. D., and others, 1950, Geologic map of the Spread Creek-Gros Ventre River area, Teton County, Wyoming: U.S. Geol. Survey Oil and Gas Inv. Map OM–118, with sections and text.

Love, J. D., Thompson, R. M., Johnson, C. O., and others, 1945, Stratigraphic sections and thickness maps of Lower Cretaceous and non-marine Jurassic rocks of central Wyoming: U.S. Geol. Survey Oil and Gas Inv. Prelim. Chart 13.

Love, J. D., Tourtelot, H. A., Johnson, C. O., and others, 1945, Stratigraphic sections and thickness maps of Jurassic rocks in central Wyoming: U.S. Geol. Survey Oil and Gas Inv. Prelim. Chart 14.

———1947, Stratigraphic sections of Mesozoic rocks in central Wyoming: Wyoming Geol. Survey Bull. 38, 59 p.

Love, J. D., Weitz, J. L., and Hose, R. K., 1955, Geologic map of Wyoming: U.S. Geol. Survey.

McKay, E. J., 1948, Red Canyon Creek area, Fremont County, Wyoming, in Wyoming Geol. Assoc. Guidebook 3d Ann. Field Conf., Wind River Basin, 1948 [geologic map in pocket].

McLaughlin, T. G., 1940, Pegmatite dikes of the Bridger Mountains, Wyoming: Am. Mineralogist, v. 25, no. 1, p. 46-68.

Masursky, Harold, 1952, Geology of the western Owl Creek Mountains, in Wyoming Geol. Assoc. Guidebook 7th Ann. Field Conf., 1954 [map in pocket].

Mead, W. J., 1920, Notes on the mechanics of geologic structures: Jour. Geology, v. 28, no. 6, p. 505-523.

Murphy, J. F., Privrasky, N. C., and Moerlein, G. A., 1956, Geology of the Sheldon-Little Dome area, Fremont County, Wyoming: U.S. Geol. Survey Oil and Gas Inv. Map OM-181.

Murphy, J. F., and Richmond, G. M., 1965, Geologic map of the Bull Lake West quadrangle, Fremont County, Wyoming: U.S. Geol. Survey Geol. Quad. Map GQ-432.

Murphy, J. F., and Roberts, R. W., 1954, Geology of the Steamboat Butte-Pilot Butte area, Fremont County, Wyoming: U.S. Geol. Survey Oil and Gas Inv. Map OM-151.

Oftedahl, Christoffer, 1953, Petrologic reconnaissance in the pre-Cambrian of the western part of the Wind River Mountains, Wyoming: Norsk Geog. Tidsskr., v. 32, no. 1, p. 1-17.

Osterwald, F. W., 1961, Critical review of some tectonic problems in Cordilleran foreland: Am. Assoc. Petroleum Geologists Bull., v. 45, no. 2, p. 219-237.

Pakiser, L. C., and Steinhart, J. S., 1964, Explosion seismology in the Western Hemisphere, in Research in geophysics, v. 2, Solid earth and interface phenomena: Massachusetts Inst. Technology Press, p. 123-147.

Parker, R. B., 1962, Precambrian agmatites of the Wind River Range, Wyoming: Wyoming Univ. Contr. Geology, v. 1, no. 1, p. 13-19.

Phillips, D. P., 1958, Geology of the Sheep Ridge area, Hot Springs and Fremont Counties, Wyoming: Wyoming Univ. unpub. master's thesis.

Powell, J. D., 1957, Geology of the Blackrock Ridge area, Hot Springs and Fremont Counties, Wyoming: Wyoming Univ. unpub. master's thesis, 118 p.

Prucha, J. J., Graham, J. A., and Nickelsen, R. P., 1965, Basement-controlled deformation in Wyoming Province of Rocky Mountains foreland: Am. Assoc. Petroleum Geologists Bull., v. 49, no. 7, p. 966-992.

Rich, E. I., 1962, Reconnaissance geology of Hiland-Clarkson Hill area, Natrona County, Wyoming: U.S. Geol. Survey Bull. 1107-G, p. 447-540.

Richmond, G. M., 1945, Geology and oil possibilities at the northwest end of the Wind River Mountains, Sublette County, Wyoming: U.S. Geol. Survey Oil and Gas Inv. Prelim. Map 31.

Richmond, G. M., and Murphy, J. F., 1965, Geologic map of the Bull Lake East quadrangle, Fremont County, Wyoming: U.S. Geol. Survey Geol. Quad. Map GQ-431.

Rohrer, W. L., 1966, Geologic map of the Kisinger Lakes quadrangle, Fremont County, Wyoming: U.S. Geol. Survey Geol. Quad. Map GQ-527.

——1968, Geologic map of the Fish Lake quadrangle, Fremont County, Wyoming: U.S. Geol. Survey Geol. Quad. Map GQ-724.

Sanford, A. R., 1959, Analytical and experimental study of simple geologic structures: Geol. Soc. America Bull., v. 70, no. 1, p. 19-51.

Sitter, L. U. de, 1956, Structural geology, 1st ed.: New York, McGraw-Hill Book Co., Inc., 552 p.

Stephens, J. G., 1964, Geology and uranium deposits at Crooks Gap, Fremont County, Wyoming: U.S. Geol. Survey Bull. 1147-F, p. F1-F82.

Thompson, R. M., Love, J. D., and Tourtelot, H. A., 1949, Stratigraphic sections of pre-Cody Upper Cretaceous rocks in central Wyoming: U.S. Geol. Survey Oil and Gas Inv. Prelim. Chart 36.

Thompson, R. M., Troyer, M. L., White, V. L., and Pipiringos, G. N., 1950, Geology of the Lander area central Wyoming: U.S. Geol. Survey Oil and Gas Inv. Map OM-112.

Thompson, R. M., and White, V. L., 1952, Geology of the Conant Creek-Muskrat Creek area, Fremont County, Wyoming: U.S. Geol. Survey open-file map.

——1954, Geology of the Riverton area, central Wyoming: U.S. Geol. Survey Oil and Gas Inv. Map OM-127.

Tourtelot, H. A., 1953, Geology of the Badwater area, central Wyoming: U.S. Geol. Survey Oil and Gas Inv. Map OM-124.

——1957, Geology, pt. 1 of The geology and vertebrate paleontology of upper Eocene strata in the northeastern part of the Wind River Basin, Wyoming: Smithsonian Misc. Colln., v. 134, 27 p.

Tourtelot, H. A., and Thompson, R. M., 1948, Geology of the Boysen area central Wyoming: U.S. Geol. Survey Oil and Gas Inv. Prelim. Map 91.

Van Houten, F. B., 1964, Tertiary geology of the Beaver Rim area, Fremont and Natrona Counties, Wyoming: U.S. Geol. Survey Bull. 1164, 99 p. [1965].

Willden, Ronald, 1965, Seismic-refraction measurements of crustal structure between American Falls Reservoir, Idaho, and Flaming Gorge Reservoir, Utah, in Geological Survey research 1965: U.S. Geol. Survey Prof. Paper 525-C, p. C44-C50.

Williams, M. D., and Sharkey, H. H. R., 1946, Geology of the Bargee area, Fremont County, Wyoming: U.S. Geol. Survey Oil and Gas Inv. Prelim. Map 56.

Wilmarth M. G., 1938, Lexicon of geologic names of the United States (including Alaska): U.S. Geol. Survey Bull. 896, pts. 1 and 2, 2396 p.

Wise, D. U., 1963, Keystone faulting and gravity sliding driven by basement uplift of Owl Creek Mountains, Wyoming: Am. Assoc. Petroleum Geologists Bull., v. 47, p. 586-598.

——1964, Microjointing in basement, middle Rocky Mountains of Montana and Wyoming: Geol. Soc. America Bull., v. 75, no. 4, p. 287-306.

Woodward, T. C., 1957, Geology of the Deadman Butte area, Natrona County, Wyoming: Am. Assoc. Petroleum Geologists Bull., v. 41, no. 2, p. 212-262.

Worl, R. G., 1963, Superposed deformations in Precambrian rocks near South Pass, Wyoming: Wyoming Univ. Contr. Geology, v. 2, no. 2, p. 109-116.

——1967, Taconite and migmatite in the northern Wind River Mountains, Fremont, Sublette, and Teton Counties, Wyoming: Wyoming Univ. unpub. Ph. D. dissert., 130 p.

Yenne, K. A., and Pipiringos, G. N., 1954, The Cody Shale and younger Cretaceous and Paleocene rocks in the Wind River Basin, Fremont County, Wyoming: U.S. Geol. Survey Oil and Gas Inv. Chart OC-49.

Zeller, H. D., 1957, The Gas Hills uranium district and some probable controls for ore deposition, in Wyoming Geol. Assoc. Guidebook 12th Ann. Field Conf., Southwest Wind River Basin, 1957: p. 156-160.

CPSIA information can be obtained
at www.ICGtesting.com
Printed in the USA
LVHW022327260821
696242LV00013B/755